POLITICAL EDUCAT
AND DEMOCRACY

Tom Brennan

CAMBRIDGE UNIVERSITY PRESS
Cambridge
London   New York   New Rochelle
Melbourne   Sydney

Published by the Press Syndicate of the University of Cambridge
The Pitt Building, Trumpington Street, Cambridge CB2 1RP
32 East 57th Street, New York, NY 10022, USA
296 Beaconsfield Parade, Middle Park, Melbourne 3206, Australia

First published 1981

Printed in Great Britain at the
University Press, Cambridge

Library of Congress catalogue card number: 81-9952
British Library Cataloguing in Publication Data
Brennan, Tom
Political education and democracy.
1. Political science – study and teaching.
– Great Britain
I. Title
320'.07'1041 JA88.G7
ISBN 0 521 28267 5

For Alice

Contents

Preface

PART I   BACKGROUND

Preface

This study is intended as a contribution to the ongoing discussion of the nature and role of political education in Britain. It attempts to sketch, in outline, the development of ideas about education for citizenship over the last century with more detailed attention being paid to the rather different conceptions which have been advanced in the last decade. An effort has also been made to identify and comment upon the barriers to further development.

I wish to express my appreciation of the assistance received from a number of friends in the Politics Association. I am particularly indebted to Professor Ian Lister of the Department of Education, University of York, who has not only helped to encourage and sustain my interest in this field over a period of years but has also given guidance to ensure that the study was kept within manageable proportions. Others who have indirectly and unknowingly contributed include Professor Bernard Crick, Birkbeck College, University of London, who was largely responsible for conceiving the Programme for Political Education and getting it off the ground, and Derek Heater, Brighton Polytechnic, who has pursued many interests similar to my own and has never hesitated to share his thought and work with me. My debt to these and other writers in the field including Harold Entwistle, Alex Porter, Geoff Whitty and others will be obvious from the text.

I have been active in the Politics Association since its inception in 1969 and have had the honour to be its Chairman from 1979 to 1981. I was a member of the Working Party which was responsible for the Programme for Political Education, the assumptions and findings of which figure prominently in the discussion. This book is, in part, a tribute to the work of the Association but it is essentially a personal statement. Where the analysis and recommendations differ from those of the Hansard Society group they should be regarded as a personal expression of opinion only.

It should, perhaps, be added that I am neither a sociologist nor a political scientist and I can only hope that in making use of sociological and political writing I have not offended against the canons of these disciplines too grievously. If the book assists in keeping alive what I believe to be the vitally important discussion on the nature and purpose of political education in a democratic society it will have served its purpose.

Tom Brennan

April 1981

Part I Background

1 Education and the polity

'To say that education reflects the values of the political and social order is, to my mind, a truism, something true for all societies, not a dramatic and specific unmasking of bourgeois–capitalist society.'

Bernard Crick (1977)

'It is a complacent, perhaps even a self-satisfied society that ignores the political education of its growing generation of young citizens. Those countries, like the U.S.A., that strive for social cohesion; those, like the Federal German Republic, that need to construct a new political consciousness; and those, like the Soviet Union, that are built on an ideology which must be sustained – all recognize the weighty significance of political education.'

Derek Heater (1978)

Political education and society

Political education cannot be considered in isolation. It is part of the wider processes of schooling and socialisation which are intimately linked with the nature of society itself. The spheres of human organisation and activity which we refer to as 'society', 'politics' and 'education' do not exist independently of each other but are, on the contrary, closely intertwined and reciprocally related. All educational systems reflect the social and political values of the dominant groups within the society which it is their function to serve and this is true for democratic and non-democratic societies alike. In some the link is more manifest than in others but in all the essential nature of the relationship is the same (see Crick, 1977).

The roots of political behaviour, and its attendant consequences for the political order, are likely to be found in childhood experiences and these tend to be more or less systematically shaped. It is not suggested that subsequent modifications of behaviour cannot and do not occur but the fact that strong social and political pre-dispositions are created in childhood needs to be recognised. It is for this reason that ruling groups in society and the institutions and processes which directly or indirectly sustain their objectives have been mindful of the importance of inculcating attitudes, beliefs and values favourable to the maintenance and development of their particular regimes. Institutional forms do not endure by their own momentum: they are attitudinally sustained.

Dewey's definition of education as 'the sum total of the processes by means of which a society transmits its acquired power and aims with a view to sustaining its own continuous existence and growth' has considerable validity. The link between school and society has been recognised by a long string of influential thinkers and it can be readily identified in works such as Plato's *Republic*, More's *Utopia* and Rousseau's *Social Contract*. The common element in all of these is the emphasis on the use of the educational system to encourage stability and harmony in the existing social order.* Thus, Plato's recommended pattern of social control was thorough and rigid. Each of the four classes within his Republic was to have a clearly designated position within a hierarchical structure and its members were to be educated in accordance with their intended station in life. Education would instil 'a spirit of order' and a 'reverence for law' which would 'attend them in all their doings' (Plato, 1945, p. 56).

St Thomas More and Jean-Jacques Rousseau, both architects of utopian communities, echoed Plato in emphasising the necessity of early indoctrination. Rousseau's *Social Contract* stressed the need for 'guidance' in order to produce 'harmony' (Rousseau, n.d., p. 132). But it is in his 'Consideration on the Government of Poland' that we find the most specific formulation of his acceptance of the need for political education in order to achieve societal objectives. He wrote: 'It is education which must give souls a national formation, and direct their opinions and tastes in such a way that they will be patriotic by inclination, by passion, by necessity.' (p. 176.) In similar vein, St Thomas More had earlier set out in *Utopia* his prescription for effective socialisation. Teachers, he said, must 'use very great endeavour and diligence to put into the heads of their children while they yet be tender and pliant, good opinions and profitable for the conservation of the public weal. Which when they be once rooted in children do remain with them all their life after, and be wondrous profitable for the defence and maintenance of the state of the commonwealth, which never decayeth but through vices rising of evil opinions.' (More, n.d., p. 132.)

* For an interesting summary of this theme see Jaros, D., *Socialisation to Politics.* The references to extracts from the classical literature follow those cited in Chapter 1 of that work.

Modern practice follows the ancient tradition: most industrialised countries and many developing nations make explicit provision for forms of political education which are designed to instil attitudes and responses that are supportive of their own political structures. As two American authors surveying the international scene observe, 'each system tries to imbue the young, implicitly or explicitly, with its particular notions of authority, legitimacy, the role of the citizen, and of the good life; at the same time it tries to present negative interpretations of politically alien systems.' (Kazamias and Massialas, 1965, quoted in Jackson, 1973, p. 21.)

Thus, the German Democratic Republic (East Germany) has its *Staatsbürgekunde*, which is a specifically designed programme of instruction followed by children from the 7th class onwards (see Mitter, 1972). In the German Federal Republic (West Germany), the education authorities in the various *Länder* provide programmes under such titles as *Politische Bildung* (Political Education), *Politische Erziehung* (Civic Education), and *Gemeinschaftkunde* (Study of Society). In France similar programmes are timetabled as *instruction civique* (Civic Education). In the USA, forty of the federal states require by law that some form of political education will be undertaken in all high schools (see Mehlinger, 1967). In the Soviet Union, the formal provision for political education for all children is supplemented by a variety of youth organisations which serve to reinforce commitment to Soviet Communism. In the Soviet Union also, no less than ten per cent of the preparatory course for all primary school teachers is devoted to political and ideological studies, including History of the Communist Party of the Soviet Union, Marxist–Leninism, Political Economy and Scientific Communism. In his efforts to transform Tanzania into a 'socialist and self-reliant' nation, the President, Julius Nyerere, recognised that the people living in the villages would have to learn how to exercise power. He observed: 'The popular belief that people will take up power and responsibility as soon as it is offered to them is not true... People have to be educated in the democratic process.' (Gauhar, 1979.) In an almost literal sense Nyerere is known in Tanzania as 'Mwatimu', the teacher.

In Britain, the nature and practice of political education has been much less overt than in other countries but it exists nevertheless and it will be argued that its effect has been to produce from the bulk of the nation's children a conformist citizenry playing minimal political roles. In British political democracy the electorate is nominally sovereign and considerable lip-service is paid to the notions of social justice, equality and participation but the prevailing political culture legitimates a political system in which there is an enormous gulf between the rhetoric and the reality of social justice and political participation. The political process perpetuates a manifestly unequal society in which the occupants of the bulk of major political roles are recruited from a relatively small section of society. What has been stressed in British society and its schools are the virtues of the 'representative' model of democracy in the tradition of Bagehot and Burke, while the possibilities inherent in the 'participatory' model in the tradition of John Stuart Mill, Rousseau and G. D. H. Cole have been ignored (see Pateman, 1970 and 1979). In the development of the post-war Welfare State the preoccupation has been with institutional structures and procedural forms rather than sensitivity and responsiveness to individuals and community groups.

Political education in Britain

For a long period the discussion of political education was almost totally neglected but more recently, following a decade of patient but persistent pressure by a small group of committed academics, educationalists and teachers, working through the Hansard Society for Parliamentary Government and the Politics Association (the professional association of teachers of politics in schools and colleges of further education founded in 1969), the case for overtly and systematically developing political studies as an integral part of the curriculum of secondary schools in Britain has been articulated and developed. Necessary research was undertaken with the aid of a grant from the Nuffield Foundation and the case for action was most notably advanced in a report on a Programme for Political Education prepared by a working party under the chairmanship of Professor Bernard Crick and published under the title of *Political Education and Political Literacy* (Crick and Porter, 1978). The presentation of the final report had been heralded by a number of articles and reports in both the 'quality' and the 'popular' press and, on publication, it received widespread and generally sympathetic coverage by the media.

Towards the end of 1974–9 Parliament, the call for political education was taken up by a number of Ministers, Opposition spokesmen and MPs, some perhaps concerned by the erosion in support for the traditional parties and some, certainly, disturbed by the degree of political ignorance, apathy and alienation among young people which recent surveys had revealed (see Stradling, 1977) and the apparently growing disenchantment with the traditional political system.* Additionally, some powerful contributors to the 'Great

* Politicians who made considered statements sympathetic to the development of political education during this period included James Callaghan, Shirley Williams,

Debate' on education including the CBI and the TUC as well as professional organisations of teachers voiced the need for a greater degree of social and political awareness, although it must be said that the assumptions made and views about the purpose to be served by such an awareness were widely disparate. The relevance and urgency of these issues was heightened by reports that the National Front had been seeking to spread its doctrines to young people through propaganda activities in schools. In this situation, professional pressure, reactions to anti-democratic rumblings and, in some cases, a straightforward desire to preserve the *status quo*, combined to create a climate in which the case for political education could be seriously examined.

Although the new interest in political education was in some instances suspect, the recommendations made in the Hansard Society report were positive and marked a decisive departure from the conformist conception. It is true that they reflected strongly the liberal–democratic tradition but there was emphasis on developing the understanding of real issues, participation was to be encouraged and there was a clear recognition of the possibilities and limitations of political action. Whatever the weaknesses of these proposals, they opened up the possibility of laying foundations upon which an education for citizenship in a democratic society could be based.

The major preoccupation in the recommendations was with the need to develop 'political literacy' which was viewed as 'a compound of knowledge, skills and attitudes' which are politically relevant. The report states: 'To have achieved political literacy is to have learnt what the main political disputes are about, what beliefs the main contestants have about them, how they are likely to affect you and me. It also means that we are likely to be disposed to do something about the issue in a way that is at once effective and respectful of the sincerity of others and what they believe.' (Crick and Porter, 1978, p. 13.) Educationally, it was suggested that the achievement of political literacy by young people would involve the practical understanding of a framework of basic political concepts drawn from everyday life and language. These would be gradually acquired and refined through an examination of problems and issues relevant to the lives of the young people concerned. It was also suggested that, attitudinally, the emphasis should be upon the cultivation of *procedural values* consonant with the ideals of democratic society, including freedom, toleration, respect for truth and respect for reasoning.

Margaret Jackson, Neil Kinnock, Christopher Price, Norman St John Stevas, John Selwyn-Gummer and Alan Hazelhurst. A more hostile view was advanced by Rhodes Boyson (see Chapter 5).

But this was not to be merely a disguised form of education for the social and political *status quo*. The Working Party identified three different objects of political education

'which are often seen as political alternatives, and as mutually exclusive:

(a) The purely and properly conserving level of knowing how our present system of government works, and knowing the beliefs that are thought to be part of it.
(b) The liberal or participatory level of development of the knowledge, attitudes and skills necessary for an active citizenship.
(c) Beyond both of these lies the more contentious area of considering possible changes of direction of government or of alternative systems.

The Working Party took the view that all three aspects should figure in the political education programme. They also suggested that 'underlying any theory of political education and any ideal of political literacy, there must be a theory of politics'. The theory they accepted is broader than the conventional view of politics in two main ways:

(a) It stresses that politics is inevitably concerned with conflicts of interests and ideals, so that an understanding of politics must begin with an understanding of the conflicts that there are and of the reasons and interests of the contestants; it cannot be content with pre-occupations of constitutional order or of a necessary consensus....
(b) It stresses that the differential distribution of power there is in any society and the differential access to resources. Here we are concentrating on a whole dimension of human experience which we characterise as *political*... (Crick and Porter, 1978, pp. 33–8)

Earlier, Harold Entwistle had argued for a form of political education based on the immediate experience of the pupil in the school visualised as a micro-political system. He rejected theoretical studies and merely simulated experiences as being inadequate and argued that the preparation for life in a political democracy is best achieved by identifying limited areas of school life in which pupils can actually *practise* responsible government. He wrote: 'We have to recognise the limitations of mere didacticism in political education. In citizenship training, as with teaching any skill, we have to recognise the importance of learning by doing. The practise of any skill is a necessary condition of how to perform it effectively.' (Entwistle, 1971, p. 103.) Entwistle's book was a notable pioneering effort which raised important questions. It articulated some of the problems of political education and castigated the 'quietism', 'legalism' and 'utopianism' which at that time still characterised the teaching of Civics and British Constitution. It did not lack a 'theory of politics' but was open to the charge that it relied too heavily on the development of political consciousness in school environments which were extremely hierarchical in structure and dominated by the values of the existing social and political order.

Others have been concerned that a meaningful political education should go beyond mere cognitive understanding and equip young people with the tools to cope effectively with the problems they are likely to meet in their own communities. Lawrence Freedman, for instance, observed: 'Political Studies should encourage an ability to ask political questions about the phenomena that students observe around them, and a sensitivity to questions of power, especially as it relates to the circumstances of their own lives.' (Freedman, 1974, p. 10.) This seems to have something in common with the aims of Bachrach and Baratz (1970) to correct the existing 'mobilisation of bias' so that less privileged groups can be helped to see the relevance of politics and use the 'political system for their own benefit' and also with the notion of 'the politics of the environment' developed in the Report of the Political Education Research Unit at the University of York, which is discussed in more detail in Chapter 6 (Lister, 1978b).

Both the Hansard Society proposals and the Entwistle approach raise questions about the possibility of an important discrepancy between intention and realisation. Moderate reformers in this field have stressed or taken for granted the need to accommodate to the traditional pattern of consensus and have embraced the values of neutrality and tolerance. More radical critics, however, have not always seen such values as universally beneficial. Herbert Marcuse, for instance, has advanced the concept of 'repressive tolerance' and argued that 'what is proclaimed and practised as tolerance today, is, in many of its most effective manifestations, serving the cause of oppression'. He delineates a *passive* tolerance of 'entrenched and established attitudes and ideas even if their damaging effect on man and nature is evident' and an *active* or *official* tolerance 'granted to the right as well as to the left, to movements of aggression as well as movements of peace, to the party of hate, as well as that of humanity'. He speaks of the abuse of tolerance which allows 'the systematic moronization of children' and which operates in a manner determined and defined by 'institutional inequality'. In this sense, he believes, tolerance is extended to 'policies, conditions, and modes of behaviour which should not be tolerated because they are impeding if not destroying the chances of creating alternative forms of existence' (Marcuse, 1976, pp. 301–4).

Karl Mannheim, in his search for a new form of democratic society which would avoid the excesses of both fascism and an unbridled system of *laissez-faire*, poured scorn on what he considered to be the

mistaken virtue of neutrality in education. He also defined strict limits
to the freedom to be allowed to those who sought to overthrow
democratic institutions (Mannheim, 1943). Aspects of Mannheim's
thoughts are discussed further in the final chapter.

In trying to bring about political, social and educational changes
in a democratic society, a situation in which there is the maximum
degree of consensus about the nature of the changes to be made is
clearly preferable to one in which there is widespread discord. There
is always the possibility, however, that friction will be avoided only
if the agreement reached is superficial and cosmetic. Such
understandings are unhelpful because they raise false expectations
and the sought-for changes are unlikely to be realised. John White
has made the important point that, in this kind of situation, the
consensus must go beyond mere 'minimalism'. The task of radical
reformers, he suggests, is to persuade others of the merits of the
scheme proposed. It must be 'the fruit of a dispassionate reflection
of the educational needs of the community or it is nothing'
(J.-P. White, 1979, p. 174). Any radically based scheme of
political education must, if it is to be successfully implemented,
take these considerations into account.

A bogus innovation?

There are some critics who exhibit clear signs of uneasiness or
cynicism about the consensus approach and who see the proposals
put forward in the Programme for Political Education as well-meaning
but doomed to failure because they can, as it were, be absorbed by
the educational system without any fundamental changes being
made. Political literacy is designed to enhance the political competence
of the mass of the people and it is impossible to forecast the outcome
of such a change if it were in fact to be brought about. But it must
be supposed that one possible outcome is that those previously most
disadvantaged may seek a more equitable distribution of goods and
resources and, perhaps, press for a system which allows more
involvement and participation. Whether or not this is a real possibility
and not a mere rhetorical flourish may be a good test of the
relevance and genuineness of any new pattern of political education
being developed.

Critics such as Ted Tapper and Brian Salter do not share the
optimism about the possible effects of the Programme for Political
Education which is felt by at least some of its supporters. These
writers are 'more than sceptical' about its capacity to achieve the
aims generally agreed let alone to bring about a more fundamental
restructuring of society. They regard it as a bogus innovation because

it fails to challenge in any significant way the social class inequalities which they believe to be inherent in the structure of British society and which are, in their view, perpetuated by the educational system. They deny the capacity of the school, by itself, to act as an agent of social change, and they state:

The conceptually-oriented approach to political education is to all intents and purposes a curriculum content innovation: a different kind of politics course designed to take the place of 'British Constitution'. As such it will compete for its place within the curriculum alongside the more established school-based subjects. Attempts to increase pupil participation in the decision-making processes of the school rest on the assumption that the school is a micro-political institution. This may be so but it is a micro-political institution with a well-defined power structure that has been legitimated by the wider society. Either pupil participation is a sham (which is invariably the case), or it relates easily and willingly to the existing power structure (which means fully legitimating inegalitarianism), or it causes an almighty turmoil when it tries to extend effective power to school students. To direct the pupil to the local community and to the issues therein that intrude upon his well-being, may be an interesting avenue for political education to take but it must relate to the internal power structure of the school if it is to be effective. (Tapper and Salter, 1978, p. 83.)

Tapper and Salter conclude that political education, 'like social education...is in danger of being labelled as an attempt to place class control on a firmer and more subtle basis' (p. 84). This fundamental criticism is in line with the kind of analysis developed by writers in the tradition of Marx, Althusser, Gramsci, and, more recently, Bowles and Gintis and others who take the view that the educational system is one of the main instruments of social control the effect of which is to perpetuate the economic and cultural hegemony of the dominant groups within society, viz. those who own and control the major resources of wealth and privilege. (See e.g. Bowles and Gintis, 1976).

If this analysis is valid, it raises important questions for those concerned with the development of political education because, although some would regard it as defeatist and put their faith in the possibility of gradual change to a more open and egalitarian society, it cannot lightly be dismissed. There is much evidence to show, for example, that educational changes since 1944 have done little to improve the relative position, educationally and economically, of working-class children. John Westergaard and Henrietta Resler (1976) argue convincingly that the postulated withering-away of inequalities of income, status and power has not materialised and that the alleged progressive transformation of capitalism into 'post-capitalism' is intellectually and empirically untenable. Tapper and

Salter do, however, concede that the pressure for the introduction of a new and more clearly articulated form of political education 'is bringing out into the open a sensitive and controversial topic – the political biases of formal education. It is asking that the connection between education and politics – which has been swept under the carpet for decades, to the point where some deny that it even exists – be reformulated and placed on a formal footing within the curriculum.' (Tapper and Salter, 1978, p. 85.)

Criticism of the proposals for political education and political literacy came from both left and right. On one hand, political education was seen as a subtle device for bolstering up a decaying capitalist system and, on the other, as a left-wing plot to destroy the fabric of British society. The Politics Association was, in the first few months of its existence, the subject of scrutiny and suspicion not least by more reactionary observers. In spite of the widely recognised professionalism and integrity of its first Chairman, Derek Heater, and the well-known patriotic loyalty and constitutionalism of its first Secretary, Colonel Frank Benemy, Lord Arran saw fit to describe it as a 'socialist conspiracy'. Both of these more extreme reactions carry with them the possibility that the proposals made were perceived in the light of preconceived positions. But, at least, the recommendations were not ignored; and the controversy they engendered underlines the inescapable fact that the nature and purpose of political education can only properly be considered in relation to the wider social and political context to which it relates.

Political education and democracy

It will be argued that education need not necessarily be directed towards the conservation of existing arrangements but that it could, subject to certain important conditions, be constructively directed towards a pattern of political and social change which places greater emphasis on the ideals of social justice. All too frequently political culture has been viewed as a static concept but to do this is to distort reality because society is dynamic not static. The process of change is continuous: there are within the political culture tensions and tendencies which can be either intensified or resisted. This point is well made by the American writer Lionel Trilling who submits that 'A culture... is nothing if not a dialectic.' It is '...not a flow nor even a confluence; the form of its existence is struggle or at least a debate' (Trilling, 1953, p. 20). Politics, suggests S. H. Beer, is 'a struggle for power, but a struggle that is deeply conditioned by fundamental moral concerns' (Beer, 1965, p. xii).

It is accepted that education alone cannot significantly alter the basic structure of society but conceivably it could be a powerful and persuasive contributory agent, especially if the alternative is seen as the progressive disintegration of political democracy, a possibility for which the present levels of political ignorance, cynicism and alienation signal a salutary warning. A case will be advanced that, ultimately, the preservation and strengthening of political democracy, which in value terms is taken as a desirable end, can only be achieved if the educational system and other social agencies make a serious effort to heighten the general level of social and political awareness, to increase the possibilities of political involvement and to seek especially to develop in young people attitudes, knowledge and skills which will enable them to be politically sensitive and, if they choose to act, politically effective.

While paying proper regard to our political and cultural inheritance such an education must encourage an active consideration of further development and possible alternatives; existing conditions and structures must not be taken as immutable. Political and social change might sensibly be taken as inevitable and even embraced as necessary and desirable. Some more radical educational commentators have seen this clearly and accepted the implications. John White, for example, in indicating the relevance of what he calls a 'practical understanding' of political and social affairs in the curriculum, writes: 'Whatever its contents it must not leave students with the idea that they must work within existing social institutions to attain their own and others' ends: it must allow them to see that existing institutions may and sometimes should be altered or removed.' (J. P. White, 1973, p. 57.) John Hipkin believes that a modern curriculum involves 'changes in political consciousness' and that the study of our cultural inheritance should be viewed not 'as the dead weight of tradition but the means by which we regenerate ourselves and our collective institutions' (Hipkin, 1976).

Such a change in educational, governmental and societal practices might serve two important purposes. It might encourage a renewal of respect for a democratic system which is increasingly being brought into question and provide 'the tools for informed and responsible participation' (Hennessy and Slater, 1978, p. 256). By creating favourable conditions for the development of social and political insights and providing the skills for citizens to pursue desired social and political objectives, it might also make a significant contribution to the realisation of the ideal of social justice in a progressively developing system of political democracy.

Within the concept of democracy, ideals and institutions are closely connected. It is true that the notion of democracy is notoriously prone to the smokescreen of rhetoric and that, thus far, there has been a considerable gap between rhetoric and reality; but properly conceived, as Benn and Peters suggest, democracy is 'not merely a set of institutions like universal suffrage, parliamentary government, and decisions by majority procedure, but also a set of principles which institutions tend to realise' (Benn and Peters, 1959, p. 355). It should also be added that institutional arrangements are subject to change and it is not beyond the wit of man to change organisational structures in such a way as to make them sensitive to the pleas and preferences of the public which they are formally designed to serve. Neither are representative and participatory models of a political system necessarily mutually exclusive; both elements could be systematically incorporated in the kind of democratic structure that is visualised here.

The American philosopher John Dewey was one of the leading exponents of the democratic ideal in education, but his convictions are relevant to the nature and purpose of the wider political system. For Dewey, democracy was a moral idea, implying a political system superior in form and purpose to other political systems. He saw democracy as an attempt to embody in society the principle that each individual possesses intrinsic worth and dignity. Democracy, in his view, implied a society in which the welfare of individuals was of the highest important and institutions were to be designed and developed with this end in view (Dewey, 1915 and 1916). If serious attempts were to be made to transform this academic possibility into practical reality, the whole political process would have to be 'conducted within the framework of moral criteria' (Benn and Peters, 1959, p. 352). Within it, political education would have a vital role to play.

In the chapters which follow an attempt is made to face up to some of the major problems, attitudinal and practical, educational and professional, which are raised by proposals for developing political education in schools. Chapter 2 attempts some ground-clearing by way of an excursion into some of the relevant sociological data on political culture and political socialisation; Chapter 3 presents a brief historical survey of the nineteenth- and early twentieth-century attitudes to political education; and Chapter 4 deals in much more detail with developments in political education over the last ten or eleven years. In Part II the kind of democratic society for which political education is to prepare the rising generation of citizens is examined and consideration is given to the many barriers which stand in the way of such a development, given the will to pursue it.

2 Political culture and political socialisation

'I lay great stress on political culture as one of the main variables of a political system and a major factor in explaining the political behaviour of individuals, groups and parties.'

Samuel H. Beer (1965)

'One of the basic assumptions underlying both political education and political socialisation is that the learning of behaviour has important implications for stability and thus for change. If the state, through a planned programme of political education, can induce citizens to act in ways which help to ensure the stability of the political order, then presumably the state can also modify these programmes to change individual behaviour patterns and perhaps the nature of the political system.'

Ted Tapper (1978)

Culture and socialisation

In examining the ways in which different societies have initiated young people into their particular styles of life, sociologists and anthropologists have used the concepts of *culture* and *socialisation*. The classic definition of culture, used in the sociological sense to refer to the total way of life of a society, is that of Sir Edward Tylor, who wrote: 'Culture is...that complex whole which includes knowledge, belief, art, morals, law, custom, and any other capabilities or habits acquired by man as a member of society.' (Tylor, 1871, p. 1.) The tendency in the use of this term is to emphasise the dominant characteristics of a society which form a *pattern* distinguishing it from other societies. It is suggested that such a pattern of life is, to a greater or lesser extent, shared by all members of a particular society and that its principal chracteristics and attitudes are transmitted to succeeding generations through the process of socialisation.

The term socialisation embodies all the ways in which the young person, through interaction with the members of his family and other social groups such as school, church, neighbourhood and peer group, learns and adapts to the forms of belief, behaviour, social norms, political values, moral principles, etc., which are favoured and stressed in his society. Frederick Elkin states: 'We may define socialisation as the process by which someone learns the ways of a given society or social group so that he can function within it.' (Elkin, 1960, p. 4.) The socialisation process is essentially conservative and it invokes strong pressures in the form of rewards and punishments to induce conformity to the attitudes and values of the group in which an individual is reared. Socialisation is the handmaiden of culture; it ensures continuity by transmitting approved norms and values.

Lawrence Stenhouse observes:

The life of any group depends upon a core of common culture. From the understanding shared in this culture, people develop a set of expectations about how others will behave, and they rely on these expectations to regulate their own behaviour. Accordingly, the group meets conformity to expectations with approval and reward, that is with positive sanctions, and responds to breaches of conformity with disapproval and punishment, or negative sanctions. (Stenhouse, 1967, pp. 18–19.)

The culture which is transmitted through the socialisation process consists, Salvador Giner suggests, of 'a relatively integrated set of ideas, values, attitudes and norms of life which possess a certain stability and this entails a learning process which takes place through human interaction.' (Giner, 1972, p. 80.) G. H. Bantock, who lays great stress on the importance of individuality, nevertheless acknowledges the powerful impact of the individual's cultural setting. He writes:

Our culture, for good or ill, exercises a powerful influence over us. It organises the way in which we see the world in these important areas of our understanding... Of course, we all add an individual and unique element to that understanding but we are still very much at the mercy of what our culture teaches us about life. (Bantock, 1968, p. 2.)

Children growing up in different societies live in different social environments and therefore acquire different patterns of culture. Illustrative examples of these differences are provided by the work of anthropologists such as Margaret Mead and Ruth Benedict. Margaret Mead, in her classic studies, *Coming of Age in Samoa* and *Growing up in New Guinea*, showed that young people growing up in these societies did not experience the stress and anxieties of adolescence which are such a marked feature of Western industrialised societies. Her work makes it clear that adolescent conflicts in complex societies are culturally, not biologically, determined (Mead, 1942 and 1943). Ruth Benedict, in her study of North American Indian tribes reported in *Patterns of Culture*, contrasts the cultural attitudes of two ethnically related groups. One group, the Zuni, attach value to personal dignity, restraint, gentleness, generosity and self-effacement: the other, the Plains Indians, condone aggressiveness, self-assertion and self-indulgence. Again it is argued that the important behavioural differences are culturally determined and transmitted (Benedict, 1968).

Sub-cultures

The impact of culture on individual group behaviour is clearly seen in the examination of the socialisation process in relatively simple, homogeneous societies of the kind studied by Margaret Mead and Ruth Benedict. It is argued, however, that the analysis of more complex industrialised societies shows that much the same kind of forces operate, although the inter-relationships are much more complex and there are significant variations in the selection from culture transmitted in different social groups. The greater diversity of complex societies implies that the forms of socialisation are also differentiated.

In the British context, it is obvious that a miner's son brought up in South Yorkshire who attends the local secondary school is reared in a social environment quite different to that of the son of a wealthy industrialist who spends term-time at one of the major public schools and vacations in Tunbridge Wells. Both share in some fundamental aspects of the totality of British culture but the way in which these features are individually experienced will be significantly different. If, for example, deference is a characteristic of British culture (see below) then there must be some individuals or groups to whom others defer. The two young people referred to here experience, as it were, different sides of the same coin; they respond to the same phenomenon but their responses are differentially and reciprocally related. The recognition that there are significant variations in the attitudes and behaviour of different groups within the same culture does not necessarily detract from the validity of the culture–socialisation argument although it does emphasise that in modern industrialised societies the process of cultural transmission is much less inclusive than that in simple, preliterate societies.

There obviously exists within the British culture a variety of distinctive *sub-cultures* based on social class, sex, region, religion, ethnic groups, etc., and the way in which the pattern of national life is perceived and transmitted will vary in accordance with the social environment in which the different sub-cultures are embodied (see Henriques, 1952; Frankenberg, 1966; Klein, 1965). So far as political perceptions and attitudes are concerned it seems likely, for reasons discussed below, that social class differences are of over-whelming importance.

Criticisms of culture–socialisation approach

At this point it must be said that this type of sociological approach in which man is viewed 'as locked into a network of social relation-ships' and as responding to external pressures which push him to act mainly in accord with the norms and standards characteristic of his time and place (Inkeles, 1964) has been subjected to strong, and sometimes strident, criticism. Dennis Wrong (1961) dubs this as 'the over-socialised conception of man' and the educator and literary critic, William Walsh, in referring to Margaret Mead's comparison between the peaceful Arapesh and the aggressive Mundugumor in *Sex and Temperament in Three Primitive Societies*, has spoken scathingly of the 'Arapesh–Mundugumor hypothesis' which falsely assumes 'an infinite plasticity of human nature' (see Walsh, 1959.) However, a recognition of the powerful effect of one's culture does not imply an acceptance of the idea that the socialisation process is completely deterministic or that inherited social structures must be passively accepted. One of the main arguments of the present book is that man does not merely adapt to his environment but is capable of adapting the environment to himself. In this context it is worth reminding ourselves that one of the basic assertions made by Aristotle was that man is a political animal who 'can act upon his environment in concert with his fellow men, not simply re-act' (Crick, 1977). Cultural forces are exceedingly powerful but the pace and direction of social and political change rest in the hands of man himself and not in the blind forces of an unpredictable fate. The important question is whether such adaptation is to be for the benefit of a small elite minority or for the welfare of the community as a whole.

Culture is an inclusive concept referring to a social entity but it does not imply absolute uniformity or immutability. Not all socialising influences are equally powerful: they can be usefully categorised into primary and secondary influences. Primary influences, such as those transmitted through the family, dispose individuals to perceive the world and to act in a particular way, but behaviour so moulded may be modified by secondary influences such as education and active membership of political organisations. These processes need careful consideration in the political context because they determine the development of political attitudes and political behaviour and thus the degree of involvement in the affairs of the body politic.

The political culture

Political attitudes and behaviour are intimately linked with the political culture. Robert Dowse and John Hughes assert that: 'The political culture is the product of the history of both the political system and the individual members of the system and, thus, is rooted in public events and private experience.' In this sense, they suggest, 'the development of the concept of political culture is an attempt to bridge the gap between psychological interpretations of individual political behaviour and macro-sociological analysis. It therefore represents an effort to return to the studies of the total political system without losing sight of the benefits of individual psychology.' (Dowse and Hughes, 1975, pp. 227–8.) This is an ambitious undertaking and one probably capable of being achieved only imperfectly because the links between the totality of a complex political system and the behaviour of individuals and groups can only partially be observed and are extremely difficult to identify and express with precision. Nevertheless, the effort to make valid generalisations has to be made if judgements on the 'proper balance between governmental power and governmental responsiveness' (Almond and Verba, 1963, p. 341) which is alleged to be one of the major characteristics of political democracy are to be made.

We may regard political culture as that part of the general culture which is concerned with the political system. It is concerned with how the system is viewed by individuals and groups and the roles which they expect to play within it. The notion of political culture embraces those assumptions, attitudes and values which are politically relevant. 'The political culture of a nation consists of the characteristic attitudes of the population towards the basic features of the political system.' (Rose, 1976, p. 1.) Politically as well as socially there is a common core of expectation accompanied by different behaviour on the part of different groups. The varying sets of behaviour largely complement each other, e.g. there are leaders and followers, powerful and powerless, behaviour may be active or passive. Which category the individual falls into is largely determined by the circumstances of his social environment and the process of socialisation. L. W. Pye submits: 'For the individual, political culture provides controlling guidelines for effective political behaviour, and for the collectivity it gives a systematic structure of values and rational considerations which ensures coherence in the performance of institutions and organisations.'(Pye, 1965, p. 7.)

Homogeneity, consensus and deference

In a general study of British government and politics, R. M. Punnett states that the three most commonly cited characteristics of the British political culture are 'homogeneity, consensus and deference' (Punnett, 1976, p. 3). To what extent do these characteristics constitute, today, a valid description of the British political culture? These characteristics and ideas, to some degree, overlap but an attempt will be made to isolate them as far as possible, for the purposes of discussion, looking first at the notion of homogeneity. Among the factors which Jean Blondel, Richard Rose and others suggest as contributing to political homogeneity are Britain's relative smallness in size, its insularity, common language, continuity of political institutions, urbanisation, speedy communications, the absence of major religious and ethnic cleavages, and the absence of a peasant class living apart from the rest of the community (Blondel, 1975; Rose, 1974). Blondel states that 'Britain is the most homogenous of all industrial countries.' (Blondel, 1975, p. 20.)

Comparative studies reinforce this analysis but, as Punnett observes, 'To place two great an emphasis on British homogeneity is to oversimplify the nature of British society.' (Punnett, 1976, p. 15.) There are significant variations within the wider culture based on region, religious, ethnic and class groupings, and recent experience, particularly in relation to the growth of nationalism in Scotland and Wales, the disturbances in Northern Ireland and the accentuation of racial tensions, suggests that these divisions are increasing rather than decreasing.

The situation in Scotland underlines the kind of duality of culture within which a major region of the United Kingdom can be significantly differentiated from the remainder of the country yet, at the same time, be bound to it by administrative, economic and attitudinal bonds. J. G. Kellas argues convincingly that Scotland constitutes a distinctive political system with a political culture different from that of England, but Scottish nationalism notwithstanding, the feeling of 'Scottishness' is modified by the reality of links with Britain. He suggests that 'Political man in Scotland stands on two legs, one Scottish and one British, and both are needed if he is to remain upright.' (Kellas, 1975, p. 18.)

The consensus view of politics in Britain is strongly represented in the literature. Rose, for example, contends that, in England, 'there is a consensus of support for the institutions of the regime and compliance with the basic political laws... while Englishmen do not agree about who should govern, they agree about how their governors should be chosen' (Rose, 1974, p. 137). The political consensus, it is suggested, is based on what Sidney Low called 'a system of tacit understanding' (Low, 1914, p. 12); and the Earl of Balfour, in writing the introduction to a new edition of Bagehot's *The English Constitutions* in 1927 went so far as to assert that 'it is evident that our whole political machinery presupposes a people so fundamentally at one that they can safely afford to bicker' (Balfour, 1927, p. xxiv).

Punnett suggests that the consensus is most marked 'in the general acceptance of the main features of the Constitution, with Parliament, the electoral system, the legal system, and the principles of Cabinet Government being accepted by the overwhelming majority of the British people' (Punnett, 1976, p. 22). This view is confirmed by the research undertaken in connection with the Granada *State of the Nation* series. To their surprise, these investigators found that 'the majority of the public express a consistently high level of satisfaction with Parliament and their own M.Ps. Citizens in Scotland and Wales seem just as happy with Parliament as the rest of the community.' (Lapping and Percy, 1973, p. 14.) The argument is advanced that the vast majority of the British people are essentially moderate and conservative and satisfied with the existing social and political order, although whether the same result would be obtained in the current climate of economic recession and widespread unemployment must be open to doubt. Punnett points out that the difference in the rhetoric of the parties is greater than the difference of performance in office and that both of the major parties have settled for the continuation of the existing political structure. It is suggested that the fundamental political consensus arises from a situation in which the mass of the electorate is, basically, satisfied with the political system and, in spite of superficial signs to the contrary, deferential towards its leaders (Punnett, 1976, pp. 22–8).

The classic statement purporting to explain the nature of political deference was advanced by Walter Bagehot in 1867. He distinguished between what he called the 'dignified' and the 'efficient' elements of the Constitution. The 'dignified' elements were exemplified by the Monarchy and the pomp and ceremony which accompanies so many of the procedures of Parliament; the 'efficient' elements, on the other hand, comprise those persons, mechanisms and procedures through which the really important political decisions are taken including, for example, the Prime Minister and the Cabinet. Bagehot believed that 'the mass of the English people yield a deference rather to something else than their rulers. They defer to the theatrical show of society.' (Bagehot, 1963, p. 248.) It is being suggested here that, like Plato's unfortunate cave-dwellers, the mass of the people mistake the shadow for the substance and that their preoccupation with the externals of political procedure allows the real decisions to be taken without fundamental criticism. This may seem to denigrate the intelligence of the electorate unduly but much the same point has been made more recently by an MP noted for his grassroots origins and contacts. Joe Ashton, in his political novel, makes his fictitious long-serving Labour MP say in a discussion about the effectiveness of Parliament: 'We have the public performances and the three-ring circus because democracy demands that the public and the vultures see what is going on. So the government put on a show, a diversion, an amusement, a bun-fight to take the attention of the mob away from the real issues... But the real power and the real arm-twisting is exercised elsewhere.' (Ashton, 1977, pp. 198–9.)

The deference thesis is supported, *inter alia*, by the fact that constituency Labour Parties, even in predominantly working-class areas, are increasingly prone to select as their parliamentary candidates Old Etonians, middle-class lawyers and academics rather than working-class trade unionists. In the period since 1945 the Parliamentary Labour Party has become increasingly 'embourgeoisified' (see Butler and Kavanagh, 1980, and earlier studies in this series). Some working-class voters have been dubbed by R. T. McKenzie as 'deferential'. According to McKenzie, the 'deferential' voter prefers political leaders of socially superior origins, views political outcomes which benefit the working class as deriving from the paternalistic acts of an elite group, regards the Conservative Party as more patriotic than the Labour Party, and prefers continuity to change (McKenzie and Silver, 1968; see also Nordlinger, 1967).

There is, however, much contrary evidence which suggests that this picture of a satisfied, deferential citizenry must be substantially modified if it is to accord with the complexities and trends of modern political reality. McKenzie himself points out that the deferential voters he describes tend to be older rather than younger and women rather than men; he suggests that 'secularism' in voting, which involves a much more pragmatic assessment of the political and economic situation, is likely to displace deference as the basis of working-class Conservatism in Britain. Later studies indicate a decline in the earlier pattern of 'solidaristic' support for the major parties and an increasing propensity towards pragmatic voting (Crewe *et al.*, 1977).

Disillusion with democracy

It is salutary to note the findings of H.McClosky who, writing of the USA, suggests that the values usually considered fundamental to our way of life, e.g. belief in freedom, democracy, constitutional and procedural rights, tolerance, and human dignity, are more widely shared and held more strongly among people in positions of leadership, influence and high status than among less favoured groups (McClosky, 1968). From an earlier survey of secondary-school pupils in England, Ted Tapper provided evidence that the highest concentration of political apathy was in the bottom streams of secondary modern schools (Tapper, 1971). It would appear that the traditional ethos of the lower-grade schools placed little premium on political competence. Results of more recent surveys on political attitudes in this country suggest that, far from a widespread satisfaction with the British political system, reactions of disillusion, cynicism and alienation are affecting increasing numbers in the community. The Report of the Royal Commission on the Constitution contained a chapter entitled 'Dissatisfaction with the Government in Great Britain' which revealed a fairly widespread disquiet about the system of government. The unease expressed was vague but deeply felt. Government was felt to be too remote and the bureaucracy was perceived as being insensitive to people's wishes and grievances. There were complaints about secrecy and an absence of effective guidance to the public on how to deal with the multitude of government organisations and inadequate machinery for appeals against administrative decisions and the remedy of grievances. The authors of a *Memorandum of Dissent*, which accompanied the main report, added: 'What is particularly disturbing is the prevailing sense of powerlessness in the face of government and the indications of a growing alienation from the governmental system.' (Kilbrandon, 1973, p. 34.) The main report observes:

We do not wish to give the impression that we have found seething discontent throughout the land. We have not. Although the people of Great Britain have less attachment to their system of government than in the past, in our opinion it cannot be said that they are seriously dissatisfied with it. But some sources of complaint which have not so far given rise to particularly rigorous or widespread protest nevertheless contain the seeds of more dissatisfaction which may arise in future if remedial action is not taken. (Kilbrandon, 1973, p. 100.)

The late John Mackintosh, who combined a professorship in Politics with membership of the House of Commons, reached much the same conclusion about the nature and extent of the modern disenchantment with government. He alleged that a

mass electorate has taken the place of the illiterate and awestruck citizenry of Bagehot's day and while the mystique of the monarchy is gone, there is the same feeling that 'they' do things to 'us'...When the electorate now pause and survey the government, they see a massive complex of authorities with no clear sign of public control, with no clear channels by which pressure can be exercised and results achieved. To put one party in power and then, four or five years later, to replace it with another seems to make little difference. Much that affects the individual can be traced to no specific persons or institutions; decisions seem simply to emerge from the machinery and local or individual complaints apparently have little effect. (Mackintosh, 1977b, p. 116.)

Social background and education

It is evident that social background and the form of education received have a marked influence on political attitudes. It is no accident that those who are educated at the major public schools and the ancient universities dominate the highest echelons of the political and administrative structures. Inequalities in the educational system have an important zoning effect on both occupational and political roles. Rose submits that:

The English educational system has always emphasised inequality...The more educational advantages a person has the more he is likely to: (i) favour the party most closely identified with the educationally advantaged, the Conservativies; (ii) show interest in politics; (iii) be active in politics.

Socialisation influences are most evidently important in the recruitment of a small proportion of Englishmen into national political roles. Those in national politics are better born, better educated and better employed than the average Englishman. As one goes up the ladder of office holder from voter to councillor, M.P., senior civil servant and minister, social differences between governors and governed increase. (Rose, 1974, p. 174.)

Tom Lupton and Shirley Wilson, in a study of 'top decision-makers', found that 50% of the Ministers included in the investigations, 19% of senior civil servants and 66% of Bank of England directors had been educated at the major public schools. Seventy-one per cent of the Ministers and 68% of the senior civil servants had studied at Oxford or Cambridge (Lupton and Wilson, 1969, pp. 5ff). Only two of Margaret Thatcher's Cabinet appointed in May 1979, did not attend a public school, one of them being Margaret Thatcher herself. Eighteen out of 22 were graduates of Oxford or Cambridge. In the House of Commons as a whole 73% of Conservative MPs, 55% of Liberal MPs and 17% of Labour MPs attended public schools. When one remembers that only 2·5% of the population attends such schools these proportions are quite staggering.

Willi Guttsman has shown that appointments to many prestigious offices such as chairmanships of Royal Commissions and Government committees, membership of the boards of nationalised industries, directorships of banks and industrial concerns, etc., far from being widely shared, are in fact restricted to a relatively small group. These are 'the pluralists of power, men who over a number of years, or occasionally even simultaneously, exert influence through a number of advising or decision-making bodies'. He adds: 'Power attracts such men and power breeds more influence and power.' (Guttsman, 1963, p. 359; see also Urry and Wakeford, 1973; Stanworth and Giddens, 1974.)

This sharp division between a political elite and the mass of the citizenry undoubtedly has close connections with the differential processes of socialisation and education. But the differences are not only those of social class; in a male-dominated political society sex is also an important factor in divisiveness. Rose writes: 'Socialisation experiences affect the political division of labour. English children learn early that people differ from each other; gradually these differences become recognisable in political contexts. Any young person not only becomes aware of differences between political parties and political roles, but also of the part he is expected to play in politics.' (Rose, 1974, p. 147.) There is differentiation and discrimination based on sex, family and social class. 'Within the home,' says Rose, 'boys and girls learn about differences in sex roles; these are potentially significant politically. Only about 12% of local councillors are women and about 4% are M.Ps.' (see Rose, 1974, pp. 148–9.)

Family influences are strong both in terms of party allegiance and in propensity towards political activity or passivity. This is illustrated by the presence of 'political' families in British politics. Seven of the 18 Conservative Cabinet Ministers appointed by Mr Heath in 1970 had family ties with politics, as had 15 out of 23 Ministers outside of the Cabinet. Increasingly the same phenomenon can be discovered in Labour parliamentary circles; in Harold Wilson's first list of ministerial appointments in 1964, 10 of 43 named had parents sufficiently involved in public life to merit notice in their own biographies (Rose, 1974, p. 147). In the Parliamentary Labour Party at this time were three sets of first-generation MPs who were brothers and a man and wife who both received junior ministerial appointments in the course of their first Parliament. Although not yet documented, there are signs that analogous family influences operate at a much less elevated level of political activity. These examples all refer to the transmission of positive political attitudes; there can be little doubt that negative attitudes are similarly transmitted.

The fact is that the majority of adolescents, but especially those who do not achieve success by conventional academic standards, are rarely encouraged in school or elsewhere to believe that they have any significant political contribution to make. Social class, family, school and occupation, positively or negatively, tend to be mutually reinforcing influences. The *Civic Culture* survey suggested strongly that this situation is avoidable; this survey provided evidence that young people who have experience of joining in decision-making in family, school or work situations are much more likely than those who have not had this opportunity to believe that they can influence the process of political decision-making (Almond and Verba, 1963, pp. 345ff). A curriculum which aims to make provision for political education in a democratic society should provide opportunities for involvement in decision-making processes. Interest, involvement and commitment in this sphere of human activity do not arise naturally, they are the result of deliberate and planned educational strategies. As A. Dickson has pointed out: 'Commitment is a consequence – and not a pre-condition – of involvement.' (see Dickson, 1975, pp. 9–10.)

Political ignorance

Any false optimism about the level of young people's political knowledge in contemporary society was dispelled by the findings of Robert Stradling's survey. This showed that the mass of young people of school-leaving age are grossly lacking in the knowledge, skills and attitudes which are necessary for citizens to contribute actively to democratic life and are singularly ill-equipped to ensure that even their minimum civic rights are safeguarded. Almost half of the young people taking part in the survey thought that the House of Commons itself makes all the important decisions in running the country; nearly three-quarters thought that local councillors have the right to change laws passed by Parliament; one in four associated nationalisation with the Conservative Party and nearly half thought that the IRA was a Protestant organisation. He concludes: 'There is something essentially paradoxical about a democracy in which some eighty to ninety per cent of the future citizens are insufficiently well informed about local, national and international politics to know not only what is happening, but also how they are affected by it and what they can do about it.' (Stradling, 1977, p. 57.) Similar surveys of the adult population reveal that this omission is unljkely to be remedied in their subsequent experience of life (see e.g. Abrams, 1967).

Jay Blumler (1974), addressing himself to the question 'Does mass political ignorance matter?', argues that it is mistaken to suppose that less knowledgeable people are any less opinionated than the better informed and he suggests that these limited perspectives favour attempts to exert pressures on government for simple solutions to complex problems, e.g. the abolition of coloured immigration. The studies of working-class voting behaviour by R. T. McKenzie and

A. Silver (1968) give extreme examples of political naivety (see also Nordlinger, 1967) but Roy Greenslade's study of the progress of a cohort of ex-grammar-school pupils shows that simplistic stereotypes are by no means restricted to the working class (Greenslade, 1979).

Stradling believes that a democratically relevant reason for improving the general level of political knowledge and involvement is that a well-informed electorate will tend 'to make governments more accountable to it and consequently more representative' (Stradling, 1977, p. 58). It must, however, be said that there is a school of thought which sees increased knowledge and involvement as injurious to the stability of the political system (see Chapter 7). This argument, even if sociologically valid, is both morally and politically reprehensible because, in a society which purports to be democratic, it is surely the case that the political system can only be deemed legitimate if it is widely understood and accepted. As the authors of the *Memorandum of Dissent* to the *Report of the Royal Commission on the Constitution* state: 'the essence of democracy is that the ordinary citizen should be involved in the political system and should be able to participate in the decision-making process' (Kilbrandon, 1973, vol. II, p. 17). If this is accepted then the present situation must give rise to acute concern.

Ian Lister has drawn attention to the fact that during the past few years there has appeared in the Western world a series of books which contend that we are confronted by a serious crisis in the political culture and its main institutions (Lister, 1977b, p. 5). Thus, from the USA, Robert Nisbet argues that there has been a serious decline in respect for traditional political institutions and he submits that 'a broad gulf exists between citizen and government in our time, a gulf broader than any that has existed in the West since the period just prior to the American and French revolutions' (Nisbet, 1976, p. 4). It is fashionable, and probably to a large extent legitimate, to distinguish between political crisis and economic crisis but the likelihood is that the two are closely intermeshed. Anthony King (1976) has indicted that the traditional structures of government are being subjected to increased expectations at a time when they are least able to meet them. Political parties have been prone to promise more than they can deliver and this has increased the cynicism with which their utterances are sometimes received. Both politicians and public have been preoccupied with industrial production and economic rewards and this has tended to devalue aspects of life which may, in the long run, be of even greater importance. It may, fortunately, be premature to think in terms of acute political crisis but the whole political system is being subjected to unprecedented strain and there are signs of unease which should have profound implications for politicians and educators alike.

We need now, as a nation, to ask some important questions about the nature of the society we are seeking to build and to give urgent consideration to the pattern of political education which will help to sustain the values which are agreed. Traditionally, political socialisation has produced political passivity and inequality; political education must assist in reversing this trend. Socialisation and education are not synonymous; they are different processes serving different ends and a clear distinction must be made between them. Both are concerned with political perception and political learning but whereas socialisation stresses conformity to an existing situation, education is essentially concerned with enquiry, questioning, insight and activity.

Political socialisation

A major drawback to the development of political education is that, in the present stage of knowledge from research, we know very little about the pattern and problems of political learning. Until very recently the literature of political socialisation research very much reflected traditional attitudes to political participation and took as given the traditional approach to democratic theory with its heavy emphasis on the need for political stability and the assumption of minimal participation by the mass of the people. The earlier political socialisation research was largely an American product which began with Hyman's work (1959). This gave rise to a rapidly growing and extending interest in political learning which was initially heavily dependent on mass social survey questionnaires but, in its later stages, adopted more refined techniques. Major works in the field which appeared in the ensuing decade include those of Greenstein (1965), Hess and Torney (1967), Easton and Dennis (1969), K. Langton (1969) and Dawson and Prewitt (1969). The now extensive literature has been comprehensively reviewed elsewhere (see Dawson and Prewitt, 1970; Jaros, 1973) and only a few comments relevant to the consideration of the development of political education will be made here.

One of the major criticisms of the earlier work in this field was the assumption that the main function of political socialisation is to create the conditions of political stability. Thus Hyman considered that 'humans must learn their political behaviour well and persist in it. Otherwise there would be no regularity – perhaps even chaos.' (Hyman, 1959, p. 10.) The view taken of the child was unnecessarily and unreasonably restricted; he was seen as the passive recipient of the political culture. Generally, also, the earlier work assumed a narrow conception of politics. It was macro-oriented, emphasising the representative theory of democracy and concentrating on national political institutions. It ignored the participant theory of democracy and the role of pressure groups both national and local. Additionally, much of the work failed to emphasise the nature and extent of differential socialisation in terms of sex and social class.

With all its limitations, however, the earlier socialisation literature did serve to dispel some of the common misconceptions about the processes of political learning. It was established that not only do children learn politically from agencies such as the family, the peer groups and the mass media, but a degree of political awareness, however vague and uninformed, has developed before the end of the primary-school stage. Greenstein (1965), for example, found that 60% of his nine-year-old sample had developed marked party preferences. This has profound implications for political education. As Entwistle observes: 'Teachers of civics are not writing political facts and ideas upon a *tabula rasa*. They confront minds with histories, having already acquired attitudes, skills and cognitive structures which dispose them to view the political universe in ways which render only partly successful any attempt to counter the liberally prejudiced and misinformed socialisation which occurs outside the school.' He adds that the political socialisation research, however, 'tells us nothing about the possibility of a constructive approach towards the improvement of political culture in personal or social terms' (Entwistle, 1974, p. 102).

Later work, especially that of R. W. Connell (1971), took a more positive approach and made constructive use of in-depth interviews with a large sample of respondents in an effort to assess the form and impact of political learning derived from agencies such as television. This work reflects Piagetian influences in that it moves beyond the essentially *static* conception of earlier researchers and views the child as an *active* agent in the selection and arrangement of the information received from the agencies of political socialisation (see also Schwartz and Schwartz, 1975).

A further important criticism of much of the political socialisation research is the failure to distinguish clearly between socialisation and education. Sometimes the two words are used loosely and inter-changeably as if they had the same meaning, which is manifestly not the case. Entwistle even considers that, sometimes, the preference for the word socialisation in this field of study is deliberate and emphasises that: 'This explicit rejection of the concept of socialisation has implications for both the quality of political culture and the development of persons as citizens.' (Entwistle, 1974, p. 101). The necessary distinction between the two words has been well expressed by Renshaw.

Socialisation can be viewed instrumentally as a means of achieving some extrinsic social, utilitarian or vocational end – for instance getting people to conform to the norms of a particular social group or equipping an individual to function effectively as a social being...whereas those ideals and human excellences associated with 'education' in the evaluative sense are implicit in the concept of education itself. Such desirable qualities of mind as rational autonomy, critical awareness and creative imagination represent values internal to the concept; they are part of what we understand by the educated man. (Renshaw, 1973, quoted in Ward, 1974, p. 31.)

Thus socialisation, as earlier suggested, carried with it implications of passivity whereas education, as Pat White (1972) makes clear, embodies the aim of providing conditions of learning which make possible reflective intellectual activity and a conscious choice between alternatives. Education is an active intervention in the process of socialisation designed to create awareness of the nature of society and the capacity to influence its development. Studies of the political culture and political socialisation have all too frequently placed a heavy emphasis on the process of adaptation to traditional norms. The political culture is created by man but it is not immutable and could be changed by man if so desired. Hess submits that 'it is no longer effective perhaps to think of socialisation as transmitting the norms of the system, a more useful perspective is the teaching of principles which underly the normative statements' (Hess, 1968).

The slow transition from the tradition of education for political conformity in Britain to new thinking about the nature and purpose of political education for participation in a developing political democracy is examined in the next two chapters.

3 Historical perspective

'*The privately-funded so-called Public Schools in the nineteenth century and through into the twentieth century consciously prepared the ruling-class youth for government – at home and in the Empire. But the civic education of the masses remained virtually confined to the annual flag-waving ritual on Empire Day.*'

Derek Heater (1977)

'*Some explanation is obviously required of the severity of the processes of political socialisation which successfully initiate the young...into a political culture of an especially complex kind... Great reverence for, and deference to, this culture must be achieved in order to produce enough loyalty to make the mixed power system workable*'.

Guy Whitmarsh (1974)

A neglected area of study

Political and civic education in England was until recent years an almost totally neglected area of educational concern. By the mid 1960s the only systematic record of its historical development had been undertaken by a German investigator, Klaus Schleicher, whose work is still not available in an English edition (Schleicher, 1965). A little earlier, M. E. Bryant, and English historian, had written a shorter survey which appeared in a Dutch journal (Bryant, 1965). Denis Lawton and Barry Dufour in *The New Social Studies* undertook a brief sketch of related developments (Lawton and Dufour, 1973) but no detailed and definitive study of the historical development of ideas about political education has so far appeared. The purpose of this chapter is to draw attention to what appear to be some of the major considerations and stages in this development and to make a tentative assessment of the period up to 1975. The developments in the period since the founding of the Politics Association in 1969, which has had a major influence on recent changes, will be discussed in more detail in Chapter 4.

The coming of compulsory education

During the nineteenth century, the ruling classes appeared to have profound misgivings about the idea of extending education to the children of the poor, feeling that this would give access to undesirable forms of knowledge and deal a death-blow to the tradition of deference. In 1807, when the debate on Samuel Whitbread's Bill for the Instruction of Poor Law Children took place in the House of Commons, the memories of the French Revolution were still fresh in the minds of the gentry and there was a manifest reluctance to educate the labouring classes lest it give rise to revolutionary ideas. The Tory viewpoint of the time is typified by the following extract from a speech made by Davies Giddy, MP:

However specious in theory the project might be of giving education to the labouring classes of the poor, it would be prejudicial to their morals and happiness; it would teach them to despise their lot in life, instead of making them good servants in agriculture and other laborious employments. Instead of teaching them subordination, it would render them fractious and refractory...it would enable them to read seditious pamphlets, vicious books and publications against Christianity; it would render them insolent to their superiors; and in a few years the legislature would find it necessary to direct the strong arm of power towards them. (Quoted in Ottaway, 1957, p. 61.)

Political leaders representing the wealthy upper classes took an extremely conservative view of both education and government. For example, Robert Lowe, the then Vice-President of the Department responsible for education, continued this vein of distrust in the second half of the nineteenth century; speaking against the 1867 Reform Bill, on which W. E. Forster was shortly to base part of his plea for working-class education, Lowe remarked that 'working men as such might be excluded from the franchise on account of their moral and intellectual unfitness' (quoted in Ottaway, 1957, p. 60). Walter Bagehot, whose classic work on *The English Constitution* was first published in 1867, observed: 'If you once permit the ignorant classes to rule you may bid farewell to deference forever.'

The predominating rationale for the introduction of elementary education in England was its presumed connection with the quest for industrial prosperity. W. E. Forster, introducing the Elementary Education Bill in the House of Commons on 17 February 1870, said:

Upon the speedy provision of elementary education depends our industrial prosperity. It is of no use trying to give technical teaching to our artizans without elementary education; uneducated labourers – and many of our labourers are utterly uneducated – are, for the most part, unskilled labourers, and if we leave our work-folk any longer unskilled, notwithstanding their strong sinews and determined energy, they will become over-matched in the competition of the world.

W. E. Forster, who had become Vice-Chairman of the Privy Council in charge of the Education Department when Gladstone formed his first administration in 1868, was a Quaker and a radical. He was the son-in-law of Dr Thomas Arnold and the brother-in-law of Matthew Arnold. He recognised clearly the link between the political system and the provision of elementary education for the masses.

Upon this speedy provision depends also, I fully believe, the good, the safe working of our constitutional system. To its honour, Parliament has lately decided that England shall in the future be governed by popular government. I am one of those who would not wait until the people were educated before I would trust them with political power. If we had thus given them political power we must not wait any longer to give them education. (See Maclure, 1965, pp. 98–105.)

Events, however, show that Forster's faith was not shared by other powerful and influential figures of the day. Compulsory education was accepted because it was industrially and commercially necessary but fears that the extension of education would lead to an excess of egalitarianism remained. This thinking was reflected in the heavy emphasis on duty and deference which characterised the content and method of the education subsequently provided. We will see that the conformist emphasis discernible in nineteenth-century speeches was continued in official pronouncements on education well into the twentieth century.

Education for conformity

The assumption seemed to be that successful 'character-building' in the elementary schools would restrain the mass of the citizenry from radical action and socialise them into an acceptance of the norms ensuring a differential access to social status and political power. This is well exemplified by the official *Suggestions to Teachers* for 1909–10, which is patronising in tone throughout and takes sharp social divisions as natural. For pupils in the elementary schools great emphasis is placed on frugality, sobriety and obedience. There are several pages of guidance on such subjects as needlework, in which it is recommended that: 'New stitches should always be taught on waste material...sufficient opportunity should be given for practice in mending garments; but in cases where there are sanitary or other difficulties, pieces of material may be used to represent the various parts of garments needing repair.' The syllabus and notes on

'Temperance' run to nearly twenty closely printed pages and there
is a three-page preface under the signature of Robert Morant which
concludes: 'Instructions on the subject of "Temperance" should
itself be temperate and should make a sober appeal to such reasoning
capacity as a child possesses and to the ideas of decent, self-respecting
or dutiful living which every good teacher endeavours to present and
cultivate in the children under his charge.' (Board of Education,
1910, p. 126). References to 'Citizenship' are much less detailed but
the intention nonetheless is clear. The general tone is expressed in
a section on 'The Purpose of a Public Elementary School' which
states:

The purpose of the school is education in the full sense of the word: the high
function of the teacher is to prepare the child for the life of the good citizen,
to create and foster the aptitude for work and for the intelligent use of leisure,
and to develop those features of character which are most readily influenced
by school life, such as loyalty to comrades, loyalty to institutions, unselfish-
ness and an orderly and disciplined habit of mind. (Board of Education, sec.
V, p. 5.)

The scheme of work for History provided that, in the seventh
year, there should be: 'Thirty-five lessons on citizenship, local
and national; visits continued.' (Sec. V, p. 97.)

Here we have an early example of the way in which the 'hidden
curriculum' of the school encourages norms and values which have
a close fit with those of the political culture. The school figures
strongly as an agent of social and political control but the general
attitudes disseminated are supplemented by a more specific programme of instruction in Civics in order to reinforce their particular,
more political, applications. As Guy Whitmarsh puts it: 'From this
point of view, the total curriculum can be characterized as "the
covert mobilization of bias". Yet this is not enough, and there is, as
a reinforcement, a specific education for citizenship tradition in
which the covert becomes overt, that is to say there is an explicit
intention to transmit the inherited political culture and to secure for
it an ideological monopoly.' (Whitmarsh, 1974, p. 133.)

The differential access to social status and political power which
the elitist culture implies is secured by the differential political
socialisation of the rulers and the ruled. The so-called public schools
encourages attitudes which accept social and political superiority for
their pupils as normal; these young people are, through their
experiences, culturally attuned to the seeking and acceptance of
major roles in politics and society. This is because there is no tension
or discrepancy between their educational experience and their social
expectations; the attitudes encountered in schooling and their social

experience mutually reinforce one another. Tapper and Salter observe: 'It is widely recognised that the British public schools have been very effective in educating their pupils politically, and that they have accomplished this without resorting to explicit forms of political education. In a very real sense the total educational experience of the public schoolboy is political training. It is effective because it is an integrated experience.' (Tapper and Salter, 1978, p. 81; see also Wakeford, 1969 and Wilkinson, 1964.) One journalist suggests that, even in 1980, this outlook still prevails. Polly Toynbee writes: 'What is odd is that independent schools still preach a spiritual theory of leadership and superiority, a *noblesse oblige* that must further alienate them from the rest of society.' (*Guardian*, 10 November 1980.)

The nature of Civics

For the masses a totally different situation prevailed. Theirs was an education in conformity to established norms and deference to a social and political elite which the public schools, in large measure, helped to produce. The Civics lessons in the elementary schools of the late nineteenth century, and carried on into the twentieth, looked at the structure of central and local government in a mechanical and unrealistic way. The approach was legalistic and procedural, referring to consensus rather than conflict; to the individual rather than groups and the clash of party conflict was ignored. Loyalty to the Sovereign, the glories of the Empire and the responsibilities of citizenship were emphasized.

The whole effect was to depoliticize politics and present the 'Constitution' as an inert body of tradition and rules which should be accepted and revered. Harold Entwistle characterised this approach as 'quietist' and suggested that it was a form of political education which 'emphasised civic *loyalty*, a norm often considered incompatible with criticism, which seems to be 'rocking the boat'. The doctrine of government by consent and the mystique attached to the privilege of voting in...elections also seem an invitation to desist from active participation in the interval.' (Entwistle, 1971, p. 28.) Lawton and Dufour comment: 'It seemed that the young in state schools were being indoctrinated into accepting their lot and apathetically submitting to an imperfect and unjust society.' (Lawton and Dufour, 1973, p. 34.) They quote H. W. Hobart as saying earlier that working-class children were being taught to 'honour the Queen, obey your superiors. Every item which receives attention is so prepared for administration to a submissive and patient race of children that it is nothing short of marvellous that any of them, when they become

adults, break away from the old rut of submissive obedience.'
(Lawton and Dufour, 1973, p. 4; see Simon, 1965.)

No significant change was apparent in the attitudes of the educational establishment as expressed in official publications for the
greater part of the next half-century. Sir Henry Hadow, Chairman
of the Board of Education Consultative Committee's *Report on the
Education of the Adolescent* (1926) and on *The Primary School* (1938)
had himself written a book on citizenship which he defined as 'the
right ordering of loyalties' (Whitmarsh, 1974, p. 142). In this he was
representative of a whole generation of high-status educationalists
who wielded persuasive authority. Indeed, as will be shown, some
of the later pronouncements in official publications are readily inter-
changeable with earlier ones. The influence of such statements
should not be underestimated because, although the curriculum of
school in England and Wales is formally free of central direction and
control, official reports and pronouncements have an important
effect, positively or negatively, on what happens in the schools. Such
attitudes, officially expressed, reflect and convey attitudes which are,
explicitly or implicitly, condoned by the educational establishment.
Few teachers are likely to be unaffected by the climate of opinion thus
created for professional socialisation is both powerful and effective
(see Chapter 6).

The Association for Education in Citizenship

In the period between the wars representations made by liberal and
radical reformers did little to reverse this trend. The most significant
but, in the end, unsuccessful attempt to change the climate of opinion
on citizenship education arose from the establishment of the
Association for Education in Citizenship in 1934. The aim of this
organisation was 'to advance the study of and training in citizenship'
especially through the teaching of history, geography, economics and
political science. (Association for Education in Citizenship, 1935; see
Lawton and Dufour, 1973, pp. 4–5). The full story of this educational
pressure group is recorded in a well-documented article by Guy
Whitmarsh (1974).

The real founder of the Association, writes Whitmarsh, was Sir
Ernest Simon (later Lord Simon of Wythenshawe) who, throughout
the thirties, 'ran the Association in an unequal partnership with Eva
Hubback' (Whitmarsh, 1974, p. 134). Initially, at least, it had the
support of a number of prominent Liberals and Fabians including
William Beveridge, G. D. H. Cole, Harold Laski and Barbara Wootton.
'Its foundation arose out of a reaction to...the rise of Nazism, Facism
and Communism.' (p. 134.) What it sought to achieve was a more

direct and meaningful form of education for democracy through the confrontation of issues. The courses to be developed were to be 'taught by means of progressive pedagogy' (p. 135). As will be seen, the organisation attracted other individuals of prominence who were much less progressively inclined than its founders and eventually the Association was virtually taken over by a coterie of Conservative politicians and educationalists.

Whitmarsh records how the Association employed pressure-group tactics in order to gain access to the Board of Education Consultative Committee under the chairmanship of Will Spens which, in 1934, had been asked to look into the organisation of secondary education. The Association had four members on the Committee and the hope was that 'direct education for citizenship would be officially recognised and promoted by means of the published report' (p. 136). But this move met with stiff opposition. The Committee, as a whole, was impressed by the more conservative view of Dr Cyril Norwood, who was later to become Chairman of the Committee of the Secondary Schools Examinations Council which produced the Norwood Report discussed below. Norwood was a member of the Association but it is evident that he did not share its more radical objectives. The Permanent Secretary of the Board of Education, Sir Maurice Holmes, was 'against politics' in the schools which brought with it, in his view, 'the problems of bias and of teachers as agents of political parties' (p. 137).

The 'pale pink political complexion of the Association' was suspect and Spens advised Simon 'to get the Conservatives in' (p. 137). This advice was taken in 1938 and the retiring Prime Minister, Stanley Baldwin, was invited to succeed the now deceased Sir Henry Hadow as President of the Association. Baldwin agreed, subject to the condition of having someone on the Executive Committee in whom he had full confidence. This was accepted and he proposed E. J. Patterson, the Director of the Bonar Law Memorial College, which had strong Conservative associations. Whitmarsh states:

From Simon's point of view, the appointment of Baldwin, as President was part of a scheme to out-manoeuvre both the Consultative Committee and the civil servants of the Board by using their political masters as a means of foisting upon the Board a departmental committee of enquiry whose purpose would be to recommend to teachers direct education for citizenship. For this purpose a memorandum on the establishment of such a committee was circulated. It argued that democracy was imperilled and that at the secondary school level the social sciences constituted the essential cognitive element in direct citizenship education. Baldwin and Halifax said they were interested and Stanhope, the President of the Board, agreed to consider it. But this was as far as the idea got. A Minute Paper circulated in the Board argued that such a committee would raise highly contentious fundamental issues; its conclusions would be so non-committal as to be futile or so definite and prescriptive as to provoke opposition and import into the schools an atmosphere of political suspicion. (pp. 138–9.)

A further effort was made by Simon to overcome the Board's negative attitude which, it became clear, was acceptable to Baldwin but this was frustrated by the imminence of the outbreak of World War II which brought in its train an insistence on a closing of ranks and a renewed emphasis on 'loyalty to established forms'. Whitmarsh writes: 'All Simon had achieved by the time war broke out was a vague promise that a pamphlet on citizenship might be issued at some future date. Possibly this promise was the distant origin of the Ministry of Education pamphlet, *Citizens Growing Up*, which was published in 1949.' (p. 139.) (See below.) Referring to an earlier incident he concluded: 'The Association had in fact been thoroughly penetrated by the government of the day in a process of what can be termed counter-mobilization.'* (p. 138.) He submits that it was the civil servants who were largely responsible for the rejection of Simon's scheme and that Simon's political allies 'were never remotely interested in what to them was the heretical idea of an open curriculum for political education' (p. 139).

The Spens and Norwood Reports

The considerable pressure put on the Board of Education and its Consultative Committee by the Association for Education in Citizenship thus came to nothing and the Spens Report promulgated a rationale which ran directly counter to the recommendations of the Association. The Committee took the view that the direct discussion of controversial political issues in the classroom was undesirable and that, for pupils under the age of 16, the traditional approach through History and Geography should be continued. The report states:

The importance of History, and in particular of recent history, for its own sake is obvious; moreover, since with pupils under 16 the theoretical discussion of economic questions is impracticable, and the objections to the direct discussion of current political questions are considerable, recent political and economic history is the best introduction to the study of politics. Not only does it supply the necessary information, but it can be taught so as to induce a balanced attitude which recognises differing points of view and sees the good on both sides. As we have said elsewhere, it is in this way,

* Whitmarsh acknowledges that the term 'counter-mobilization' is taken from J. P. Nettl's *Political Mobilisation* (Faber and Faber 1967) 'in which the author argues that normally counter-mobilization occurs from above to prevent the social system from representing social cleaveages'.

by precept or still more by the breadth of their own sympathies, that teachers can best educate pupils to become citizens of a modern democratic country.

Geography also can give a conception of the world and of its diverse environments and peoples, which should enable boys and girls to see social and political problems in a truer perspective, and given them sympathetic understanding of other peoples. For the older pupils a comprehensive scheme of world-study, based on well-grounded principles, can offer scope for the consideration of a variety of vital problems bearing on social, economic and political life. Such a course, in our opinion, is to be preferred to the isolation of one aspect of geography, for instance, physical, political or economic geography. (Board of Education, 1938b, p. 174.)

The ill-famed Norwood Report was even more direct in its condemnation of the idea that politics and economics should be studied in the school at an early age. The report states:

Nothing but harm can result, in our opinion, from attempts to interest pupils prematurely in matters which imply the experience of an adult – immediate harm to the pupil from forcing of interest, harm in the long run to the purpose in view from his unfavourable reaction....

In this connection we wish to consider one of the many topics which have been brought to our attention for inclusion in the curriculum, namely education for citizenship. From what has already been said we hope it is clear that we regard it as of vital importance that education should give boys and girls a preparation for their life as citizens. We agree with the contention of the evidence which has reached us that British men and women should have clearer conceptions of the institutions of their country, how it is governed and administered centrally and locally, of the British Commonwealth and its origins and working, and of the present social and economic structure, and that they should realise their duties and responsibilities as members of these smaller and greater units of society. Of all this we have no doubt. But we remind ourselves that the growth from childhood to adolescence and so to citizenship is a gradual process and that, if the later stages are to be sound, the earlier stages cannot be forcibly hurried through. The practical problem is to discover how much can appropriately be taught to children at different stages of their development and how that teaching can best be given. Our own belief may be shortly put thus. Teaching of the kind desired can best be given incidentally, by appropriate illustration and comment and digression, through the ordinary school subjects, particularly History, Geography, English and foreign languages and literature. Nevertheless lessons devoted explicitly to Public Affairs can suitably be given to older boys and girls certainly at the Sixth Form stage, and probably immediately before this stage. The most valuable influence for developing that sense of responsibility without which any amount of sheer information is of little benefit is the general spirit and outlook of the school – what is sometimes called the 'tone' of the school. (Board of Education, 1943, pp. 57–9.)

The Education Act 1944

In the immediate post-war period, official references to civic education remained pious and traditional. The 1944 Act contained the first-ever statutory reference to 'education for citizenship' but this was contained in a provision never to be implemented. Section 43, dealing with the then intended scheme for the establishment of County Colleges, placed upon local education authorities the duty of educating young people in such a way as would 'enable them to develop their various attitudes and capacities' and 'prepare them for the responsibilities of citizenship'.

In succeeding official statements lip-service began to be paid to the idea of the school 'as a community' and to the task of 'educating for citizenship' but this continued to be interpreted as meaning descriptive studies of the constitutional machinery of government and the encouragement of 'civilised' personal relationships. *The New Secondary Education*, issued in 1947, stated:

The individual pupil needs to develop as a member of a community and he must learn to live with other people. The secondary school can make a deliberate effort to include a leading feature of its syllabuses and training a study of what has come to be known as 'Citizenship' or 'Civics', that is, the basic information about local and national government, rates and taxes, the judicial system, and so on. It can lead the pupil to a wider conception of his status and responsibilities as a citizen of this country and of the relation between this country and the British Commonwealth and the United Nations. (Ministry of Education, 1947, p. 15.)

In 1949, a further Ministry pamphlet, *Citizens Growing Up*, recognised the need for civic education but saw citizenship as 'a matter of character' (p. 21). It concluded: 'there are forward-looking minds in every section of the teaching profession ready to reinterpret the old and simple virtues of humility, service, restraint and respect for personality. If the schools can encourage qualities of this kind in their pupils, we may fulfil the conditions of a healthy democratic society.' (Ministry of Education, 1949, p. 41.)

The Social Studies Movement

The educational euphoria which accompanied the ending of World War II brought forth many new developments including what came to be called the 'Social Studies Movement'. As Lawton and Dufour (1973) record, it began in 1945 with the publication of *The Content of Education*, prepared by the Council for Curriculum Reform, which was an offshoot of the Association for Education in Citizenship. For Social Studies it was envisaged that there would be a 'common-core' course for younger pupils leading to more specialised courses in particular disciplines, such as history, economics or politics, in the upper school. The purpose was to develop in the pupil awareness of himself as an individual, as a member of organised groups, and as a member of a modern, industrialised society. *Inter alia*, its aim was to create 'self-reliant, participant, mature citizens' (Hemming, 1949, p. 9). Such studies were closely linked with 'discovery learning', 'the project method' and other characteristics of 'progressive education'.

For the less adventurous, Social Studies frequently became an uneasy amalgam of History and Geography under a new name. For more ambitious it represented an 'integrated' course of all relevant disciplines. The teachers' handbooks which reflected the aims of the movement made some sweeping claims. Thus, one of the leading exponents, James Hemming, proclaimed that 'a broad Social Studies course' would provide 'a core of knowledge, experience and insight around which other subjects at whatever degree of specialisation, may be built in a co-ordinated way'. One alone of the seven major objectives summarised in his book sought to foster the development of 'spontaneity, self-reliance, flexibility of mind, clear thinking, tolerance, initiative, articulateness, adventurousness of outlook, courage in the face of new problems, enjoyment of creative activity, sound standards of action and appreciation, worldmindedness, a sense of purpose, and a philosophy of life' (Hemming, 1949, p. 25; see also Dray and Jordan, 1950).

These were laudable but over-ambitious objectives and, understandably, there were difficulties in achieving them. The Social Studies Movement was idealistic in orientation but deficient in the effective execution of its intended purposes. The assault on the earlier rigidities of content and method was well-intentioned and justified but the plan to replace them lacked structure and coherence. The aims were grandiose but the teachers' skills and energies were necessarily widely diffused and the courses proved difficult to handle successfully. The sociologists and political scientists, who might conceivably have provided a structural underpinning for the course, had not yet arrived in the schools. Many head teachers were uneasy about the amorphous nature of the new development and the challenge to the old procedural certainties; teachers of the traditional History and Geography courses were anxious to reassert their lost independence. These and others pointed to the weaknesses of Social Studies and actively assisted in its demise. Social Studies suffered the fate of other curricular innovations which are, in the main, reserved for non-examination pupils. Because it was a 'low-status' activity in this sense, it failed to establish itself in the minds of teachers, parents and pupils as a desirable part of the curriculum. Subsequent developments in this field were more cautiously approached.

In spite of the manifest deficiencies of the Social Studies Movement one suspects that there were many worthwhile and successful experiments which went unrecorded, the successful and unsuccessful alike being tarred with the same brush of cynicism. The movement had some promising offshoots which are relevant to the concerns of political education. Of particular interest are fields such as 'education for international understanding' and 'world studies' (see Brennan, 1961; Heater, 1976 and 1980), which have an important relationship to the concerns of political education but which have so far, regrettably, developed independently of more directly political studies. The movement also provided the basis for the development of materials and methodological techniques which are of lasting importance.

The Crowther and Newsom Reports

A definite change in official attitudes is discernible in the Crowther Report (Ministry of Education, 1959) and the Newsom Report (Ministry of Education, 1963). Neither of these contained any systematic statement on the role of political education in the curriculum but the relevant incidental references were much more encouraging than the gloomy strictures of earlier reports. The Crowther Report asserted positively:

The fact that politics are controversial – that honest men disagree – makes preparation for citizenship a difficult matter, but it ought to be tackled, and not least for the ordinary boys and girls who now leave school at 15 and often do not find it easy to see any argument except in personal terms. (Ministry of Education, 1959, p. 114.)

The Newsom Report is vague about the kind of political education to be pursued but it did at least point to part of the problem. In a section on the curriculum entitled 'The Proper Study of Mankind', it suggested that:

A man who is ignorant of the society in which he lives, who knows nothing of its place in the world and who has not thought about his place in it, is not a free man even though he has a vote. He is easy game for 'hidden persuaders'. (Ministry of Education, 1963, p.163.)

The question of 'educating for citizenship' again came into the foreground with the preparation for the raising of the compulsory school-leaving age to 16 in the mid 1960s. The Schools Council Working Paper on this theme advocated a carefully considered programme through which young adolescents could gain 'access to a complex cultural inheritance' including 'some appreciation of the dilemmas of the human condition and the rough hewn nature of many of our institutions, and some rational thought about them' (Schools Council, 1965, p. 14). It was observed that 'older pupils will all too soon be forced to find a way of coping with a complex social, economic and political order which demands some degree of understanding of its purposes and operation' (p. 13). The document also drew attention to the 'large ideas' which members of a civilised society have to grasp: 'the rule of law, a sense of justice, a willingness to accept responsibility, an honourable carrying out of undertakings freely entered into, a sense of debt to the past and responsibility towards the future, government by consent, respect for minority views, freedoms of speech and action and readiness to recognise that such freedoms depend on trust, friendship and individual responsibility for the manner in which they are exercised. It is the large ideas which are seminal, not the details.' (Schools Council, 1965, p. 16.)

Political education and 'The Whole Curriculum'

Following a spate of publications on a variety of educational problems and concerns the Schools Council, in 1971, set up a working party to look at the curriculum as a whole in order to identify problems which all teachers face and to consider what principles should govern the selection of curriculum content. The report which resulted from these considerations, published in 1975, explores what are regarded as 'some controversial issues' and states that it is not intended to be 'prescriptive or partial'; it is noteworthy in the present context, however, because it contained the most explicit statement on political education emanating from the report of an official body connected with education up to that time. The relevant paragraphs stated:

Pupils may reasonably expect to receive a political education appropriate to participation in the life of a democratic society. The school should not advance on its authority the standpoint of any political party or the personal views of its staff. All political opinions should be subject to impartial and critical scrutiny. Schools should help pupils to understand our society as it stands and equip them to criticize social policy and to contribute to the improvement of society. (Schools Council, 1975, p. 25.)

Society may reasonably expect that schools will help their pupils gain a general knowledge of the democratic process and a respect for the law, as well as an understanding of how to participate in political processes, to change the law and defend oneself from injustice. In pursuit of these twin objectives the school should help pupils, so far as it is within its power to do so, to realise in their individual lives the paradoxical combination of conviction and tolerance of others which is fundamental to democracy. (Schools Council, 1975, p. 27.)

The report expressed the hope that 'by clarifying the issues' it would 'help teachers to make sounder judgements and decisions'. The statement was, perhaps, not entirely uninfluenced by the pressure brought to bear by the Politics Association which sought to make politicians and educators more aware of the case for the development of political education. These and other developments in the last decade are examined in more detail in the next chapter.

4 Recent developments in political education

'If one could locate countries along a spectrum of activity in civic education, Great Britain a mere decade ago would have been placed on the far edge of neglect.'

Derek Heater (1978)

'We should follow the example of the new West German universities and make political education part of the curriculum. This is, of course, no dull or small proposal. It is an important – or dangerous, some will feel – proposition about the entailment for practice of a certain kind of theory.'

Bernard Crick (1975)

The Politics Association

Before the mid 1960s evidence of a sustained official or academic interest in the place of politics in the school curriculum was hard to find. The scene in this regard was, as Derek Heater remarked, one of 'pervasive stagnation' (Heater, 1978; see also Brennan and Brown, 1975). References to political institutions and, much less frequently, political issues and problems, figured in the curriculum of some secondary schools in courses on British Constitution, Civics, Social Studies, General Studies and Current Affairs but these courses were likely to be descriptive and legalistic in character and lacking in real cognitive penetration (see Brennan, 1974).

British Constitution was established as a subject at both Ordinary and Advanced levels in the General Certificate of Education but this was taken only by a minority of pupils and it was a subject which was poorly regarded in both schools and universities. Professor Crick had such contempt for it that he remarked:

In my own experience, as a persistent first-year teacher both at L.S.E. and Sheffield...it is rarely any advantage for a student to have taken 'British Constitution' at school, often the contrary. And this is not simply because he thinks that he knows it already, but because...his mind is often astonishingly full of irrelevant and picturesque detail about parliamentary procedure and 'constitutional institutions' so that he has none of that inquisitive turbulence about the manifold relationships of ideas to institutions and to circumstances that is surely the essence of a political education. (Crick, 1969, p. 3.)

No literature dealing comprehensively with the problems and possibilities of political education in Britain existed; there was no appropriate professional association; and no colleges or departments of education offered directly relevant courses of training (see Heater, 1969b). The dead hand of the attitudes expressed in the Spens and Norwood Reports lingered on and effectively stifled any faint stirrings of professional interest. There still existed a widespread feeling in educational circles that a realistic study of politics was inappropriate for young people of school age. Anyone with an interest in changing this situation faced a daunting task, but a few dedicated individuals took on the challenge and in the course of the period from 1969 to 1980 met with considerable success.

The greatest credit for the initiation of these developments must be accorded to Derek Heater, then Head of the History Department at Brighton College of Education, and Bernard Crick, then Professor of Political Theory and Institutions in the University of Sheffield. On 14 April 1967, the *Guardian* published a letter to the editor from Derek Heater which deplored the state of political education in Britain and recommended the establishment of a new professional association to cater for the needs of teachers of politics in schools and colleges of further education. Professor Crick, who was one of the few university teachers of politics to take an interest in what was happening in political education in the schools, lent his considerable prestige and support to this venture and persuaded the Hansard Society for Parliamentary Government to arrange a conference of interested teachers which was held at University College, London, in September 1969. Thus the Politics Association was born; Professor Crick became its first President and Derek Heater its first Chairman.

The Politics Association, which relies almost entirely on the voluntary efforts of its officials and members, has always operated on a financial shoestring; aiming initially at one thousand members, it has never recruited more than six hundred. It holds an annual conference which provides a platform for prominent politicians, political scientists, educational experts and others. Prestigious speakers during the last decade have included the Rt Hon. Reg Prentice, MP, when he was Sretary of State for Education and Science in a Labour government, and the Rt Hon. Sir Keith Joseph, Bt, MP, when in Opposition. David Steel's scheduled appearance at the conference in 1976 was cancelled when he became involved in the election for the leadership of the Liberal Party. Both Mr Prentice and Sir Keith Joseph along with other leading political and academic figures gave support and encouragement to the work of the Association and helped to give it status and an image of respectability.

The Association served as a catalyst for interested teachers who had hitherto ploughed lonely furrows, with no means of identifying and communicating with other teachers up and down the country who shared their own enthusiasm and aspirations. The Association's *Newsletter* was quickly transformed into a professional journal, *Teaching Politics*; it produced a series of *Occasional Publications* and entered into arrangements with publishers for the publication of relevant A-level books for schools. Some local branches were formed but the continuation of this local activity was and is heavily dependent upon the presence and activity of enthusiastic individual members.*

From 1970, books and articles dealing with aspects of political education began to appear and a steady stream of such writing has continued to attract the attention of teachers, educationists, academics and politicians. Television and radio provided time for discussion on political education and specially prepared programmes for schools dealing with political institutions, issues and problems have been presented (see Brennan and Brown, 1975 and Heater, 1978). GCE syllabuses have been revised and new CSE syllabuses are in course of preparation. Perhaps most importantly, relevant research has been undertaken and a tentative model for 'political literacy' has been developed.

The Politics Association filled an important gap by providing a focus and a forum for the discussion and development of ideas about political education and a means through which recommendations for action could be channelled. Both the Association, formally, and its individual members, informally, ensured that publicity was given to relevant shortcomings, problems, events, and research findings. The Association for the Teaching of Social Science, founded in 1967, also began to take a systematic interest in political education, initially perhaps in a competitive spirit but more recently in a spirit of constructive co-operation (see Chapter 6).

The Politics Association, in association with its parent body, the Hansard Society, quietly but successfully employed pressure-group tactics in the pursuit of its objectives. Geoff Whitty remarks: 'This lobby...has – as one might expect from professional students of politics – displayed a remarkable capacity for getting right all the things that create a successful pressure group campaign – their

---

* The current policy of the Politics Association is presented in the statement included as Appendix I.

timings, their use of the media, their friends in high places and so on, all seem to have paid off.' (Whitty, 1978, p. 5.) This is perhaps to over-rate the degree of professional organisation in activities which were in reality more the sum of a number of unco-ordinated individual and group efforts than the product of a master plan. It has to be said that although the founding of the Politics Association was timely and its limited resources for the most part economically and intelligently applied, it would have probably been less successful in putting political education on the map if other influences had not contributed. It is always difficult to establish cause and effect in complex social processes but the coincidence in time of a number of events and circumstances with the new interest in political education suggests some interesting links between the relevant phenomena. Whatever the connection, the outcome gave a decisive boost to the advocates of a new form of political education.

Parliament and the DES

When, within a relatively short space of time in the early 1970s the legal age of majority was lowered from 21 to 18 (as from 1 January 1970) and the statutory school-leaving age was raised to 16 (1972–3), it was pointed out that even those who left school at the earliest possible date were less than two years away from the assumption of full civic rights whereas, before these changes, the gap between the two dates had been six years. This new situation led many observers and a few popular newspapers to recognise that if education for citizenship was to become a reality it must be undertaken during the last year or two at school otherwise it was unlikely to be undertaken at all.

The recognition of some of the problems of political education on the part of the political parties and the news media was highlighted by a sudden spate of publicity on the issue of a series of sixth-form conferences which were being organised by the Conservative Party. These conferences had in fact been held before this time without any notice being taken of them. Attention was drawn to the conferences in an article in *The Times* on 14 January 1973, and the story was taken up in other national and regional papers. A spokesman of the Labour Party accused the Conservatives of attempting to indoctrinate school pupils and this provided the ingredients for a political slanging match between the two major parties. The danger in this was that these events might revive the time-worn arguments about the alleged dangers of 'politics in schools' and so jeopardise the healthy developments that were beginning to take place. The matter was hastily considered by the officials of the Politics Association and Professor

Crick, the then President, drafted a series of 'ground rules' for the conduct of such conferences to which representatives of the three major parties agreed. The 'concordat' arrived at in this way was printed in full in *The Times Educational Supplement* on 2 February 1973 (see Appendix II).

The 'concordat' emphasised the need for maintaining political balance in such events and stressed the educational criteria on which their organisation should be based. It was suggested:

That politicians talking to pupils on controversial matters in school time should only do so in circumstances where they fit into a systematic programme organised by the school or a group of schools and where there has been preparation by the teachers. Isolated visits tend...to be a waste of everybody's time, and schools should not think that their responsibilities are met simply by talks from the parties: they must be prepared for and followed up by the schools.

The agreement, which was widely publicised in the press, did in fact contain a pointed commentary on the state of political education in the schools and the need for development. It said, for example:

Civic education whether in CSE, O-level or A-level syllabuses as 'British Constitution' or 'Government and Politics', or in sixth form General, Liberal or Social Studies time, is both a highly important and a difficult, hence sometimes neglected, area. It needs expansion and more thought both for its educational value and as a deliberate attempt to make young people aware of their responsibilities as citizens, which obviously must include the possibility of supporting and even joining political parties and pressure groups. We deeply fear the social consequences if over-direct approaches to schools by the parties make this whole area too controversial for schools to handle. The suppression of political controversy can lead to the rejection of politics, sometimes in forms more worrying than mere apathy. (*The Times Educational Supplement*, 2 February 1973.)

A further important consequence of this controversy and the agreement arrived at was that it firmly established the Politics Association, in the eyes of the major political parties, and probably the Department of Education and Science, as an impartial and responsible body which could speak with authority and good sense on relevant matters of educational controversy. In any event, in 1974, the DES approved a grant to the Association of £1,400 per annum for three years to assist with its organisation and development. About the same time, also, the Nuffield Foundation approved a grant of £38,000 for the establishment of a Programme for Political Education, to be sponsored by the Hansard Society in conjunction with the Politics Association. The Leverhulme Trust approved a grant of £11,000 to enable the Hansard Society to investigate the political knowledge and awareness of young people (see Stradling, 1977), and the Ford Foundation provided £60,000 for research by the Hansard Society, part of which was earmarked for the investigation of the relationship between Parliament and the public, taking into account such matters as access to the House and its members, the relations between MPs and their constituents and outside interests, media treatment of parliamentary matters, and public attitudes to Parliament and MPs. Some months later the Government awarded grants for political education to the two major youth organisations, the British Youth Council and the National Association of Youth Clubs.

One of the most convincing of the explanations for the growth of interest in political education, especially on the part of politicians, lies in the growing concern about the apparently declining levels of support for the political system especially among young people and the increasing evidence of political ignorance among the young discussed in Chapter 2. That there has been a steep decline in membership of the main political parties over the last decade is beyond question (see Leonard, 1975 and Houghton, 1976). Over the same period increased support was given to the minor parties, not least the Scottish and Welsh nationalist parties; pressure-group activity increased and more extreme political groups like the National Front and the Socialist Workers' Party received greater prominence in the mass media. Geoff Whitty notes that 'in announcing grants to the National Association of Youth Clubs and the British Youth Council..., Shirley Williams drew attention to a drift towards extremism among the young and the need to win them back to the middleground of politics'. Whitty considers that 'the apparent desire to give explicit political and industrial education can be seen as a product of the current crises of capitalism and social democracy' (Whitty, 1978, p. 5). Current concerns of this type are, in effect, perceived as worrying and unwelcome deviations from the traditional pattern of political culture which stressed conformity with the established political order.

On 26 September 1977, the *Guardian* reported that 'The Prime Minister is backing proposals now being considered by the Department of Education to fund a national investigation into why Britain's youth is becoming alienated from the political party system.' The following day the same newspaper stated: 'An all-party group of M.Ps. to examine the difficulties facing youth – including the growing problem of political alienation – is expected to be set up when Parliament returns from the summer recess.' Subsequently the Department of Education made grants to the two major bodies representing youth organisations: £20,000 was awarded to the British Youth Council on which the main political parties, together with youth organisations including Scouts, Guides and church youth

CAMBRIDGE
UNIVERSITY PRESS

have pleasure in sending for review a copy of:

Brennan: Political Education and
Democracy.

Price: £3.95 A P/B (SBN 0 521 28267 5)

Publication date _____ 15th October 1981

It is requested that no review should appear before this date.

May we ask you to let us have a copy of any review published or, if you send a copy of your journal, to indicate the pages on which a review appears?

The Edinburgh Building, Shaftesbury Road, Cambridge CB2 2RU
Telephone (0223) 312393

groups are represented; and £18,000 was allocated to National Association of Youth Clubs.

Many individuals and organisations will welcome this sign of a new interest in political education on the part of political leaders but it would be unfortunate if any of the parties involved were to perceive the function of political education merely as that of buttressing an ailing political system. Political education must imply much more than an attempt to perpetuate or rekindle the pattern of political quiescence and conformity which characterised the earlier period of development. What is required is a positive conviction about the role of political education in a developing democracy rather than a negative reaction to phenomena which appear to disturb the customary calm of political passivity.

The 'Great Debate'

That the new interest in political education was not confined to politicians became clear in the process of the so-called 'Great Debate' when a variety of powerful pressure groups – educational, religious and industrial – made their views known. The submissions to one of the four regional conferences (held at Peterborough on 11 March 1977) have been analysed by Professor Crick. The organisations concerned included the Council of Local Education Authorities, the National Union of Teachers, the National Association of Teachers in Further and Higher Education, the Headmasters' Association, the National Association of Head Teachers, the Church of England Board of Education, the National Consumer Council, the Confederation of British Industry and the Trades Union Congress.

The changing climate of opinion can be gauged from examples of a few of the more explicit statements. The submission of the National Association of Teachers in Further and Higher Education observed: 'If we are to develop greater participation in political, social and industrial life..., it is necessary for schools to equip young people to play their part. This involves a curriculum wide enough to give young people the basis for such participation.' The Headmasters' Association said: 'Included in this should be an awareness of the major social, political and moral issues which our society faces.' The Church of England Board of Education asked: 'How far is the educational system, not only "fitting" children in our society, but enabling them constructively to criticise and reshape it?' The TUC submitted that: 'If there is to be a core curriculum which all young people should share equally, then it must include a thorough preparation for playing a full part in democratic life – both political and industrial. In other words, all young people must be helped to become politically and economically literate, and understand the basic structure of our industrial society.' (Crick and Porter, 1978, pp. 7–8.)

Taken together these statements, although inevitably to some degree platitudinous, constitute a powerful body of opinion which indicates that, at least in general terms, there is a wide degree of consensus on the need for political education. In view of this widespread concern it is disappointing that the only mention of political education in the ensuing Government Green Paper was a passing reference, couched in vague terms, which acknowledged the need for a greater awareness of 'the role of the individual participating in democracy' and a recommendation that young people should 'be equipped with a basic understanding of the functioning of our democratic system, of the mixed economy and the industrial activities which create our national wealth' (Department of Education and Science, 1977). As Geoff Whitty observed: 'It was almost as if the political dimension had been added as an afterthought to a document more concerned with the relationship between school and industry.' (Whitty, 1978, p. 4.)

We have already seen that from the mid 1960s the publications of the Schools Council increasingly paid attention to the nature and role of political education, albeit in sometimes pious terms. The statement on *The Whole Curriculum* in 1975 asserted that: 'Pupils may reasonably expect to receive a political education appropriate to participation in the life of a democratic society'; and that 'schools should help pupils to understand our society as it stands and equip them to criticise social policy and to contribute to the improvement of society' (Schools Council, 1975, p. 25).

What such a political education implied was much more specifically set out in a discussion document on 'Political Competence' prepared by the HMIs, Roger Hennessy and John Slater, which was first made known to the wider educational public when it was published in *The Times Educational Supplement* on 25 November 1977, although it had been circulated privately before this time. In the document it was argued that the importance to society of political education 'requires a clearer definition of its objectives, and of the knowledge and skills and attitudes which are necessary to support it'. The document discussed the relevant content, concepts and attitudes which are deemed appropriate to 'informed and responsible participation' in a democratic society. It also recognised that school organisation and 'the pedagogy employed through the school' had political implications. It concluded: 'Political education might also do something to restore a respect for political activity and attitudes, and rescue them from the worrying trend of current cynicism about the place of politics in society.' (See Crick and Porter, 1978, Appendix B, and *The Times Educational Supplement*, 25 November 1977.)

Political literacy

A further impetus to the cause of political education was given by the publication, in the autumn of 1978, of the report of the Hansard Society's Programme for Political Education. This programme had been concerned with curriculum development and an assessment of the viability of innovations in political education which aimed at enhancing 'political literacy' in secondary schools and non-degree classes in colleges of further education.

In designing the work and assessment of the Programme, the original intention was that a small group based in London would be concerned mainly with encouraging development in political eduction and that the main task of the Political Research Unit based at the University of York would be to monitor and assess such developments. The York group were also to study examples of good teaching practice independently of the London group, and to produce detailed case studies of good teaching practice. In the event, limitations of finance, personnel and geography adversely affected the monitoring activity and both groups were, to a large extent, engaged in development work and assessment of it. This produced problems of co-ordination and there was, inevitably, some degree of overlap. The revised arrangement did, however, enable interesting comparisons to be made between the methods and findings of the two groups both of which had worked to the same set of documents and guidelines but developed somewhat different approaches. The reports of the two groups were compiled separately and, in an effort to avoid confusion between the two, the published report edited by Professor Bernard Crick and Alex Porter (Crick and Porter, 1978) is referred to as the Hansard Society Report and that from the Political Education Research Unit, under the direction of Professor Ian Lister, as the York Report (Lister, 1977b).

The proposals made in the Hansard Society Report are important not only because of their intrinsic educational and political interest but because of the impact which they have made on associated educational development. For the first time, in this country, there was available to those interested in this field of education a statement that went beyond mere platitudes and vague generalisations and presented a coherent model which was explicit about the political and pedagogical assumptions on which it was based and clear about its recommendations for practice. Since subsequent discussion in the field of political education is likely to hinge on reactions to or modifications of this model it is important to be clear about its nature and intentions and, therefore, a brief summary of its major considerations and recommendations is now made.

The Working Party did not begin with the assumption that 'political literacy' was 'best gained by teaching about politics directly' and thought it was particularly important to consider how such literacy could 'be advanced through other subjects, for instance, History, English, Geography, Social Studies and Economics' (Crick and Porter, 1978, p. 2). In the event it did not prove practically possible to test out all of these possibilities but the limited evidence provided by the field-work undertaken suggested that political literacy teaching was most successful where it had been done through courses which had 'been constructed with exclusive political literacy objectives'. It was felt, however, that this question should remain open and the Working Party expressed the need to explore further the possibility of political literacy objectives being successfully infused or integrated into courses designed to meet the objectives. The place of political education in the curriculum is discussed further in Chapter 5, but it should be made clear at this stage that whether the approach is direct (through a specially designed course of political studies) or indirect (through another subject such as History or English), the view of the Hansard Society researchers was that the syllabus should be clear about the political education objectives and that these should be given explicit attention.

As outlined in Chapter 1, political literacy is viewed as a compound of knowledge, attitudes and skills appropriate to political awareness and understanding which are to be developed together and based on a 'practical understanding of concepts drawn from everyday life and language'. In accordance with the assumptions developed in the Programme, the young person will be deemed to have achieved political literacy when he has become aware of the nature of the main political disputes and how these affect ordinary people in their everyday lives. He will also be inclined to act politically in matters which affect him or engage his sympathy rather than to accept passively the views and actions of others. The politically literate person will be sufficiently informed to defend his interests and to make his action as effective as possible but he will, at the same time recognise that others will not share his particular viewpoint and be reasonably tolerant of alternative perceptions and beliefs (see Crick and Porter, 1978, p. 33).

The political literacy approach attempts consciously to politicise the young person's experience, in accordance with a certain set of values, towards specific objectives. In order to clarify the meaning and implications further, the report poses and answers three questions:

(a) *What kinds of knowledge would a politically literate person possess?*
(i) The basic information about the issue: who holds the power; where the money comes from; how the institution in question works. (This may apply to Parliament, a committee of the County Council, a school, a trade union, a club or a family.) (ii) How to be actively involved using the knowledge of (i) and understanding the nature of the issues. (iii) How to estimate the most effective way of resolving the issue. (iv) How to recognise how well policy objectives have been achieved when the issue is settled. (v) How to comprehend the viewpoints of other people and their justifications for their actions, and always to expect to offer justifications oneself...
(b) *What are the attitudes of a politically literature person?*
...It is no part of this project to expect that all the values of Western European liberalism will be taken for granted or can be applicable everywhere. What we have inherited as part of our tradition must be subject to criticism and sometimes scepticism. There is in our view no *correct* attitude to be inculcated as part of political literacy: nevertheless attitudes will inevitably be adopted and they will be based consciously or unconsciously on values.

The report recommends that teachers of politics must adhere to a set of 'procedural values' which are accepted as necessary ingredients in political literacy. These are identified as freedom, toleration, fairness, respect for truth and respect for reasoning.

(c) *What skills would a politically literate person possess?*
The politically literature person is not merely an informed spectator; he is someone capable of active participation or of positive refusal to participate. At the same time...(he) is capable of thinking in terms of change and of methods of achieving change...We are confident that political action is worthy of encouragement if it is based on knowledge and understanding. (Crick and Porter, 1978, pp. 13–14.)

It is argued that the approach to political literacy is necessarily *conceptual* and that a politically literate person should possess vocabulary of concepts from which he or she can construct elementary frameworks for political understanding. The report states:

The concepts chosen were treated as genuinely *basic* or *primary*, that is those from which others more complex can be derived and on which theories, generalisations, explanations and moral judgements can be based. But these concepts are not necessarily what people regard as the most important or the most widely used terms. For instance, 'Democracy' is plainly a most important concept, but it is a compound of more basic concepts...

So we developed what is essentially the oldest and simplest model of politics: the perception that it is about the relationships of rulers to the ruled, the few to the many, 'them and us' and the possible relationships between them. (pp. 14–15.)

Government, it is suggested, is associated with *power, force, authority* and *order*; our identity as people can be expressed in terms of *natural* rights, *individuality*, *freedom* and *welfare*: the relationships between government and the governed can be expressed in terms of *law, justice, representation* and *pressure*.

The report also makes clear that, unlike the traditional syllabuses of which it is highly critical, the political literacy approach will not only include reference to how the existing political system works and the assumptions which lie behind it, but will also encourage knowledge, attitudes and skills appropriate to active participation and provide for the consideration of alternative political systems and the possibilities of political change. The Programme, therefore, takes account of and encourages awareness of 'the main doctrines of politics, of conservation, participation and change'. The report states: 'It is hard, indeed, to see how any account of politics can be plausible which does not draw, in different circumstances and for different purposes, on each of these three theories or doctrines.' There is, however, an important qualification; each of the three aspects the authors say is 'a perfectly proper area of educational concern, capable of treatment without gross bias, but only when taken together with some consideration of the other two...The safest generalisation...is that all three objectives must find their place in the curriculum together and not be taught in isolation, or to the exclusion of the other.' (Crick and Porter, 1978, pp. 12–13.)

It is intended that the emphasis in study and activity designed to promote political literacy should be on issues and problems rather than institutions or procedures. It is suggested that the issues to be considered could be selected from the findings of opinion polls, the media (both national and local), material from the political parties (including manifestos, election addresses and party political broadcasts), the 'politics of everyday life', and those deemed to be close to the experience of the young people chosen either by the teacher or the class itself (pp. 16–18 and 74–9).

An interesting paper by Dr R. Stradling is included in the report which argues that a structured mode of thinking about political problems and situations can best be achieved by the use of a 'spiral' curriculum on the Brunerian model, in which the central political concepts are systematically 'revisited' and reinforced at successive stages, 'firstly in simple, concrete and familiar contexts and then "spiralling" outwards to a broader framework, and building upon these ideas the structure of a given model of thought or discipline' (pp. 18 and 89–90). One example is given of how such an approach might be worked out in practice in a specially designed syllabus for developing political literacy with young people aged 14–16 years. The recommended content includes personal, school and local issues, issues of party conflict, issues of institutions (e.g. devolution, electoral reform); and issues of personal politics and ethics (including e.g. abortion, crime, industrial democracy and 'the closed shop').

Numerous criticisms have been and will be made of these proposals but they at least provide a framework upon which further development can be based. The Working Party has manifestly had a realistic concern for the need to obtain the maximum degree of political and educational consensus but did not shirk from making recommendations which involve encouraging young people to equip themselves to understand the practical working of the political system, to be aware of the differential distribution of power, and to entertain the possibilities of political change. The proposals will certainly not satisfy those who take a revolutionary view of political change and will doubtless be unwelcome to those who are attitudinally wedded to the *status quo*. But they go far beyond the conformist and quietist approach of the older tradition and, after such a long period of neglect, offer possibilities of developing realistic and meaningful political education in the schools. The proposals clearly need to be refined and developed through discussion and practical experience in an operational setting but there are already signs that they are having a significant effect on political education as it is now being developed not only in schools but also in youth and further education activities.

Ongoing research and activity

The Programme for Political Education concentrated on the development of political literacy for the 14–16-year-old age group in schools but the Working Party recognised that an equally pressing need existed in the further education sector for which there existed no body corresponding to the Schools Council responsible for funding research and development in the field of political education. In an effort to meet this deficiency the Hansard Society obtained from the Anglo-German Foundation for the Study of Industrial Society a grant of £12,600 for a period of two years to support and extend the work of the Programme for Political Education into the field of further education. A working party was set up under the chairmanship of Geoffrey Stanton of Garnett College, London, and Robert Stradling was appointed as Research and Development Officer. The particular concern of this group is with the political dimension of General and Business Courses and Industrial Studies provided in colleges of further education. The Research Officer was charged with the responsibility of conducting case-study research, co-ordinating the development of teaching materials and monitoring the use of these in the institutions co-operating in the project. The final report will be of great interest to all those concerned with the development of political education.

The grants made to the British Youth Council and the National Association of Youth Clubs has provided an opportunity for experiment in a field which has hitherto been seriously neglected so far as the official encouragement of political education is concerned. The British Youth Council has devoted its attention to the production of education 'packs' on themes such as 'Racial harmony', 'The General Election 1979', 'The European Community' and 'Working for Change'. It also intends to arrange conferences for youth leaders in the use of these packs. The National Association of Youth Clubs also hopes to develop materials for use in youth clubs and to monitor their use in order to establish models of good practice.

More or less simultaneously with the developments in the activities of the British Youth Council and the National Association of Youth Clubs, resulting from official funding, other relevant activities have been initiated by means of assistance from or endowment by voluntary bodies. The Methodist Association of Youth Clubs has launched a programme of political education. A handbook written by Dr Fred Milsom proposes three main approaches including the informal discussion of current affairs; the establishment of groups to meet specifically for more formalised political education; and participation in community action. Dr Milsom believes that too much church youth work in churches encourages naivety and pietism and takes too little account of the realities of political conflict. He writes: 'Christian optimism at its best is not founded on avoiding ugly facts: our compassion should be based on realism, and never obscure that aspect of politics which is a search for power.' This programme may be viewed as an attempt to make 'a radical return to one of Methodism's earliest practices, when members were encouraged to influence the secular affairs of society' (Milsom, 1978a). This, if successful, may go some way towards assisting the trend noted in the study of social change in south-west Wales whereby leaders of the chapels concerned themselves with matters such as Sunday observance, temperance and gambling to the exlusion of more politically contentious issues; a change which led to a decline in support from individuals and groups who attached value to a Christian view on more fundamental political issues (see Brennan *et al.*, 1954 and Milsom, 1980).

An interesting project concerned with the political education of young workers has been funded by the Leverhulme Trust for three years, and is co-directed by Philip Cohen and David Robins and based at the Department of the Sociology of Education, Institute of Education, University of London. It starts from quite different assumptions and adopts a radically different mode of operation: it is concerned with 'Political Socialisation and Working Class Youth Culture in the Inner City' and seeks to investigate the impact of different kinds of work experience in shaping the political awareness of school-leavers in this particular environment. An experimental intervention is built into the project. This consists of the establishment of informal educational groups which are designed to provide a basis for encouraging new forms of youth representation in the community, including, for example, the production of a youth newspaper and the setting up of a Young Tenants' Organisation. The project directors state: 'Instead of politics with a capital P, whether of the propaganda/recruitment variety or old style civics, students are encouraged through practical work, investigation and argument, to learn how political processes are locked into immediate problems.'

Geoff Whitty reports Cohen and Roberts as claiming that 'it is partly the result of the neglect of the young by the traditional organisations of the Labour Movement which leads to their retreat into the politics of the peer group and the attraction of some of them into organisation of the ultra right'. They argue that what is required is 'the building of new forms of youth representation, on the shopfloor, in tenants' associations and elsewhere...in which a continuing process of political education can take place, and from which progressive rank and file youth leadership can emerge' (Whitty, 1978, p. 9).

Some of the more directly pedagogical problems are touched on in Chapter 6 but it is relevant here to refer briefly to the evidence adduced by Paul Willis of a 'counter-culture' developed by working-class youngsters in the secondary school which is in part characterised by more or less systematic strategies of withdrawal from the values of the school. This situation presents a challenge to political education no less than to other parts of the curriculum; there is little doubt, however, that the solution is more likely to lie in a fundamental review of educational objectives and values than in marginal changes in methodology. Willis observes: 'These processes should not be mistaken...for mere institutional flux or localised disturbance. What is *not* supposed to go on in school may have more significance for us than what is *supposed* to go on in school.' (Willis, 1976, p. 199.) Willis makes the important point that the adoption of withdrawal strategies rather than the possible alternative of presenting challenges to the young people concerned tends to obscure the problem. He suggests that far from causing some of the serious problems at present encountered in secondary schools, the counter-culture and the processes it sponsors has helped to prevent a more serious crisis (see Willis, 1977). New attitudes and methods in education inevitably produce problems of resources, organisation and management but with all their problems, the open, positive and participative approach advocated in the Programme for Political Education and similar progressive pedagogies are surely preferable to the negative situation of negotiated withdrawal. One suspects that there is a strong similarity between the withdrawal strategies practised in the school by underprivileged groups and those engaged in politically by sections of the adult population. It is, therefore, important that this problem be viewed socially and politically as well as educationally.

Early in 1979, following discussion with the Politics Association, the Hansard Society and the Institute of Education of the University of London submitted a scheme to survey and selectively monitor current teaching practice and teacher-training schemes in political education over the next three years. A grant of £78,000 was approved by the Department of Education and Science and Alex Porter of the Institute of Education, formerly Secretary of the Politics Association, and Robert Stradling, Research and Development Officer of the Hansard Society, were appointed as co-directors. In this programme the assumption is made that political education within the formal sector of the educational system has now entered a period of innovation. It is proposed to chart these developments and to examine the implications of the different initiatives and approaches observed for the future provision and practice of political education in secondary and further education and also the provision and practice of teacher-training schemes in political education.

When account is taken of the virtual absence of constructive thought about the nature and purpose of political education only a few years ago, and the situation at that time of neglect and negative thought about the role of political education is compared with the current spate of systematic enquiry in secondary schools, youth organisations and further education, the progress made is impressive. The differing lines and forms of investigation seems to the present writer an advantage because as the Hansard Society/Institute of Education proposal states: 'to prescribe what should and should not be regarded as political education without taking account of current practice would impose unduly restrictive parameters upon the research'. There is a tendency for work in youth organisations, schools and unattached individuals and groups to proceed in separate compartments and one hopes that at appropriate stages efforts will be made to compare and contrast findings of these different investigations so as to establish the degree or absence of commonality in the relevant problems and approaches.

Political education and the core curriculum

In the 1970s, thinking on the curriculum of the secondary school within the Department of Education and Science moved first towards the acceptance of the idea of a common-core curriculum and then to the more or less open advocacy of this proposal. Demographic changes which led to falling rolls in the secondary school added weight and urgency to the discussion of this still controversial issue. The claims for political education received the ultimate accolade of respectability when 'political and social education' was specifically mentioned as an important and integral part of the curriculum in the DES consultative document, *A Framework for the School Curriculum*, published in January 1980 (Department of Education and Science, 1980b). In this, the Secretaries of State made it clear that it was their intention to seek a national consensus on a desirable framework for the secondary-school curriculum and drew attention to 'the extent to which some key subjects should be regarded as essential components of the curriculum of all pupils'. The document expressed the view that 'the curriculum, whatever subject structure may be adopted, should seek to prepare pupils for employment and adult responsibilities in society' (p. 2). The proposed core curriculum, it was suggested, should be based on the eight 'areas of experience' postulated in *Curriculum 11–16* (Department of Education and Science, 1979a), which were defined as 'the aesthetic and creative, the ethical, the linguistic, the mathematical, the physical, the scientific, the social and political, and the spiritual'. The document made the important point that all these areas were to be regarded as being of equal importance and stated that 'the curriculum should be capable of demonstrating that it offers properly thought-out and progressive experience in all of these areas'.

This statement was welcomed by the Politics Association which made a detailed response drafted by the present writer (see Appendix III). The Association used the opportunity to make clear its view of the role of political education in the curriculum and drew attention to the resource and training implications of such a development. The relevant curricular considerations are discussed further in Chapter 6.

Local education authorities

The new status given to political education in official documents encouraged local education authorities to examine the provision made for this activity in their own schools. Some did this with enthusiasm and others with varying degree of reluctance. But, as emphasised in Chapter 3, the persuasive authority of such official documents is considerable and there is little doubt that, formally and informally, prestigious members of Her Majesty's Inspectorate exercised a helpful influence. There was now a climate in which progressive LEAs could take stock of school organisation and curricular provision and this appears to have encouraged other authorities to do the same. The provision for political education has moved fastest and farthest in those LEAs who have interested and enthusiastic advisers who have harnessed the talents of interested and enthusiastic teachers. Sheffield was the first to appoint an adviser specifically for political education, in the person of Roy Hedges. Interest in the Inner London Education Authority in this field developed rapidly following the appointment of Richard Whitburn as Adviser. Notable work is being done in Northamptonshire where a Senior Adviser, Keith Driscoll, has taken an active interest and worked closely with the local branch of the Politics Association.

A consortium of LEAs in the Tyne and Wear area is actively considering the feasibility of a joint, inter-authority political education project, the aims of which would be 'to identify the problems associated with the teaching of political education in schools, to encourage the development of pilot studies in contributory schools, to evaluate what has been achieved and, eventually, to publish some validated recommendations'. If established this project is likely to receive financial assistance from the Schools Council. West Sussex has produced a report on 'Education for Living' which has a substantial section on Political Education. A very interesting interim report on *Education for Democracy and Political Education* was received by the Devon authority which included sections on The Objectives of Political Education and on methods and resources. This concluded that 'political education should not be developed by means of a sharply-defined curriculum structure taught by prescribed methods, but by the laying down of well-defined objectives accompanied by a variety of methods, which can be tailored according to the resources available in each school' (Golby and Rush, 1980). Other LEAs which have shown interest in this field by attending courses on the teaching of politics and political education or encouraging work to be undertaken in teachers' centres and in other ways include Merton, Waltham Forest, Hampshire, Hertfordshire, Hounslow, Humberside, Kent, Sefton, Berkshire, Dorset, Lancashire, and a consortium of the Glamorgan LEAs.*

* It is not suggested that this list is exhaustive. It is based on information received from a variety of sources and it is possible that there are developments in some authorities of which the writer has no knowledge.

It is, unfortunately, clear that these authorities are the exception rather than the rule. In 1977 the Department of Education and Science issued a circular to LEAs which was designed to produce a picture of 'their policies and practices in curricular matters'. The summary of replies is very revealing, not least in the field of political education (see Department of Education and Science, 1978b). In response to the question 'What steps have the authority taken to help schools promote the development in their pupils of a basic understanding of contemporary economic, social and political life?', three-fifths of the LEAs said that the issues underlying the question 'could be largely incorporated into more or less traditional subjects' (p. 160). Some authorities 'made particular mention of political education, usually expressed an awareness of the need for caution in introducing it as a separate subject' (p. 161). 'Less than one tenth of the responses indicated the authority had designated an adviser with particular responsibility for all or part of the area covered by this question.' (p. 161.)

Universities and polytechnics

Only a small minority of the universities and polytechnic institutions has made special provision for developments in political education. The University of York established a Political Education Research Unit under the direction of Professor Ian Lister which was actively associated with the Hansard Society Programme for Political Education and it maintains a very useful 'documentation service' from which interesting articles in the field are available. The Institute of Education, University of London appointed Alex Porter, formerly General Secretary of the Politics Association, as Lecturer in Political Education and the University of Birmingham appointed Clive Harber as a lecturer with special responsibilities in political education. The Department of Political Institutions and Political Theory, University of Liverpool, where Professor F. F. Ridley, the current President of the Politics Association, has been active in providing courses and conferences in the teaching of politics and political education. The City of Sheffield Polytechnic has received approval from the CNAA to offer a part-time in-service course in Political Education, and the Institutes or Departments of Education in the Univerities of York, London and Birmingham along with the Department of Politics and Sociology, Birkbeck College, London, where Professor Crick is Head of Department, all offer Master's degree courses with special options in aspects of Political Education.

GCE syllabuses in politics and government

Although an important distinction must be made between political education (with which this study is mainly concerned) and the teaching of politics as a school subject, it is significant that quite substantial changes in the content and approaches to the study of government and politics at school level, and especially in GCE syllabuses, took place from the mid 1970s. It can be reasonably inferred that these changes resulted, directly or indirectly, from the reforming zeal of those who were advocating a more enlightened form of political education: indeed it is true that in a number of cases the changes can be directly attributed to individuals who were active in the work of the Politics Association.

When the present writer surveyed the full range of GCE syllabuses in this field during 1971–2 it could be said that all the syllabuses at Ordinary level and more than half at Advanced level followed the traditional 'constitutional' approach (Brennan, 1974). Five of the eight boards offered O-level papers under the title of British Constitution, two offered Economic and Public Affairs, and one offered Economic and Public Affairs with an alternative paper on The Structure and Workings of British Government. Typically the requirement was that the working of the British Constitution should be studied 'descriptively' rather than 'analytically'. The emphasis was on the acquisition of detailed knowledge of institutions and procedures and little was expected in terms of awareness and insight into the realities of the political system. Controversial issues were avoided and questions on political parties and pressure groups did not appear at all in some of the examination papers whereas questions on the Monarchy, the Privy Council and the role of committees in local government were firm favourites. It was concluded: 'The general criticism of the existing papers at O level is that they are much too formal and encourage an approach which, because of the detailed knowledge demanded, either inhibits or prevents a study of political life which could be made challenging, realistic and revealing. Above all, they fail in the essential educational purpose of developing a fuller understanding of basic concepts which are the key to increasing intellectual awareness.' (Brennan, 1974, p. 19.) Since then there have been substantial changes in the A-level syllabuses but developments at the Ordinary level have proceeded at a much slower pace. In 1974, the Joint Matriculation Board introduced a new O-level syllabus under the title Government, Politics and Economics with a common-core paper in The Citizen and his Place in Society and an optional paper in Government. Since then the Associated Examining Board has approved a revised O-level syllabus in Government and Politics which is designed to encourage a study of both the institutions and processes of the modern system of government, the scope of governmental intervention in economic and social affairs, and an examination of the individual in the context of society and its political system. The University of London's new alternative O-level syllabus in Political Studies has two sections. Part A covers British Central and Local Government, with Part B offering optional studies in Industrial Relations, Control of the Media and other relevant thematic studies.

Of particular note among the A-level syllabuses are those of the Northern Universities Joint Matriculation Board, the Oxford and Cambridge Schools Examination Board, The Associated Examining Board and the University of London. The Joint Matriculation Board syllabus in British Government and Politics was in many ways a pace-setter although it must be observed that initially this was more apparent in the questions set than in the syllabus as formally presented. When the majority of boards still retained the traditionally arid British Constitution approach, the Joint Matriculation Board perspective was much more in line with the way that Politics was developing as an academic discipline. Even when it still had the title of British Constitution questions were set on voting behaviour, the nature of party conflict and the representation of organised interests, as well as matters of current controversy. Rather different in character, but also distinctive, was the Oxford and Cambridge Schools Examination Board syllabus in Political Studies. This offered four papers: I. Political Thought; II. Representative Government; III. British Constitutional History since 1830; IV. Theory and Practice of Government. Candidates were required to take any two of Papers I, II and III with IV being a 'special' paper. Paper I was designed to test understanding of the major concepts in political thought (e.g. the state, sovereignty, authority) with a selection of classical texts ranging from Rousseau's *Social Contract* to the *Encyclicals* of Leo XIII to serve as the basis of study. Paper II was concerned with the working of political institutions in Britain and the USA. Paper III required reference to general developments in the political system as well as the legal framework of institutions.

A new Associated Examining Board A-level syllabus in Government and Politics was introduced in 1974 to replace the traditional offering in British Constitution. This was unusual in having a compulsory Paper I, under the title of Political Behaviour – Britain, which was predominantly sociological in character. This required knowledge of the concept of political culture and its applications; a study of the literature on voting behaviour, pressure groups, elitism v. pluralism, and some consideration of organisation and political power and the nature and conditions of political and social change. Paper III initially gave three options in the study of Political Institutions; candidates could choose Britain *or* the USA *or* the USSR. The syllabus proved to be very popular with enthusiastic and committed teachers of politics; some welcoming the opportunity to examine the British system both institutionally and sociologically, others being attracted by the possibility of looking in some detail at an alternative political system.

Perhaps the most striking of all A-level syllabuses currently in operation is the University of London syllabus in Government and Political Studies, for which Professor Bernard Crick is the Joint Chief Examiner. This consists of a compulsory Paper I on Political Institutions and Concepts with optional papers in Modern British Politics; Modern Political Ideas and Doctrines; Public Administration; and Comparative Government. The new syllabus is based on three assumptions:

(i)   that it is a better reflection of the diversity of approaches to the study of Politics in British Universities and Polytechnics than the existing syllabus in British Government and Political System, hence the need for optional papers which emanate from a compulsory core paper;
(ii)   that an 'A' level in 'Government and Political Studies' can and should fulfil both the demands of civic and political education and of preparation requirements for specialised undergraduate studies;
(iii) that any change must not be too drastic since some teaching of politics in both schools and Colleges of Further Education is being undertaken by non-Politics graduates and this may continue for some time. (University of London, 1977, pp. 1–2.)

These aims not only reflect current thinking in the teaching of politics in schools and colleges of further education but recognise the reality of the educational situation in which the work is to be undertaken.

As the *Notes of Guidance for Teachers* makes clear this syllabus has been influenced by some of the ideas of the Hansard Society's Programme for Political Education but in this context it is the academic rather than the 'political literacy' objectives which guide the examiners in assessing the papers (University of London, 1977, p. 4.) Nevertheless, there is a commendable emphasis on the academic value of knowledge of current political concerns. The notes states:

Certainly in Paper I and in the Public Administration option of this syllabus, a candidate who neither reads a quality newspaper nor listens to Radio 4 can only hope to obtain a high grade if he has quite extraordinary knowledge, and even then he is unlikely to do as well as a candidate who reads a good newspaper and follows the better current affairs programmes on radio and television. (p. 4.)

Not all boards have yet moved away from the limitations and constraints of the traditional constitutional approach but the general

Candidates entered for A-level Politics, 1970–9[a]

	1970	1971	1972	1973	1974	1975	1976	1977	1978	1979
Associated Examining Board[b]	2088	2330	2639	2555	2152	2392	2488	2661	2760	1435
Cambridge[c]	—	—	—	—	—	—	—	—	52	98
Joint Matriculation Board	2815	1959	1791	1627	1369	1506	1736	1677	1688	1851
London	3796	3826	3868	3876	3576	3305	3592	3414	2456	2826
N. Ireland[c]	—	—	—	—	—	—	—	55	138	168
Oxford	568	628	679	636	573	660	630	747	797	854
Oxford and Cambridge[d]	361	302	294	286	241	247	257	280	258	251
Welsh	90	158	162	214	255	364	456	417	437	415
Totals	9088	9203	9433	9194	8166	8474	9159	9251	8586	7990

[a] The boards were asked for information on Summer entries only. Associated Examining Board, Joint Matriculation Board and London made clear in their replies that the information was for Summer entries only. For the rest, I think it can be safely assumed that they do not run a second examination.

[b] Home candidates only. The Associated Examining Board's overseas entry is roughly similar, however. Thus, after rising to a peak of 201 in 1978, overseas entries fell to only 92 in 1979.

[c] Before the inception of their specialist syllabuses, both of these Boards offered Politics at A-level in combination with Economics.

[d] Excludes entries in Economic and Political Studies, which have regularly been three times as large as entries in Political Studies alone. It should be noted, however, that entries in the integrated examination have dropped slightly more sharply than in Political Studies, from 1206 in 1970 to only 782 in 1979.

Compiled by G. Berridge, Department of Politics, University of Leicester and published in: Grassroots, no. 24, Politics Association, September 1980.

trend is markedly in the direction of a more conceptual treatment which encourages a realistic appraisal of current issues and problems, a realisation of the complexities and limitations of government, and an awareness of the relationship between political ideas, institutions and processes. A fuller development of this kind (but one which desirably retains some differences in the avenues of approach) will not only result in a more realistic and rewarding pattern of political study but will bring about a greater degree of congruence between political education and the more academic study of political and government in the secondary school.

The table showing the pattern of candidates entered for the A-level examinations in political subjects for the period 1970–9 suggests that the introduction of new, more intellectually demanding syllabuses induces an initial fall-off in the number of entries but the indications are that the earlier upward trend in entries is likely to be restored.

It is obvious that much progress has been made in political education and in the teaching of politics as an academic subject during the last decade. In the field of political education, however, many problems and barriers to further development remain. The nature of these problems is examined in some detail in Part II.

Part II Barriers

5 Traditional attitudes and professional hostility

'Our opposition to the National Front must not blind us to the Pandora's Box of problems and disputes which could be opened by political education in the schools. It really is time politicians and other adults solved their own problems instead of once again pressing them on to schools, like an unwanted Christmas present.'

Rhodes Boyson, MP (1978)

'The expression "political education" has fallen on evil days; in the wilful and disingenuous corruption of language which is characteristic of our time, it has acquired a sinister meaning.'

Michael Oakeshott (1962)

Problems and barriers

In advancing its claim for the development of political literacy, the Working Party responsible for the Programme for Political Education was conscious that it was seeking an important educational change. It was, at the same time, concerned to obtain the maximum political and educational support for these proposals because it believed that they could only succeed if there was a reasonable degree of consensus about the need for such a change. To some extent it succeeded in this purpose: the proposals received a good press and there were expressions of goodwill and support from leading politicians and educators. The proposals did not, however, command the immediate sympathy and support of the wider spectrum of politicians and teachers; in some cases, indeed, the reception was extremely hostile. In spite of what many observers regarded as the positive and constructive tone of the Hansard Society recommendations there was sharp criticism from both right and left whose representatives, for different reasons, were sceptical about the Programme's intentions and probable effects. There were also expressions of extreme unease from a number of individual politicians and teachers as well as from some professional organisations. The fact that some of these criticisms were ill-informed did nothing to decrease their vehemence.

Some of the critics occupy influential positions and signs of unspoken hostility to the venture from various sections of the educational world remain. Those who espouse the cause of political education, therefore, would be wise not to underestimate the opposition to their plans or to minimise the problems, pitfalls and barriers which stand in the way of their future development. The fate of the former Association for Education in Citizenship (see Chapter 3) provides an important historical lesson and current efforts for reform must take careful account of the reactions of those who do not accept the need for a new form of political education. Many of the barriers are attitudinal and stem from deep-seated convictions about the nature of society and what the individuals and groups concerned deem to be the necessary and proper emphases in educational activity. Other problems relate more directly to educational matters such as school organisation, teaching methods, resources and training. Some barriers and problems lie within the nature and institutions of society itself.

In order to examine these problems more systematically an attempt is made to formulate a number of broad categories or groupings into which individual problems appear to fall. It will be obvious that these are categories of convenience and not procrustean divisions for there are, inevitably, overlaps and linkages between them. The grouping below is advanced only tentatively and is followed somewhat flexibly but it is suggested that those concerned with the development of political education might sensibly have regard to the following types of barriers.

1. *The barriers of conservatism.* These are attitudinal and stem from the existence of a strongly entrenched conservative tradition in education and society.

2. *Professional barriers.* These are variously based but some of the most important are associated with groups having conflicting or even complementary interests.

3. *Pedagogic barriers.* These include the problems of school organisation, curriculum innovation, methodology, teacher training and resources.

4. *Societal barriers.* These include problems which arise from:

(a) the lack of congruence between the objectives of political education and the actual assumptions and practices of social and political institutions and organisations (e.g. the political literacy programme encourages the 'procedural values' of freedom, toleration, fairness, respect for truth and respect for reasoning, but these are not universally respected).

(b) the inhibitive effect of certain values inherent in the political culture (e.g. conservatism, deference, and the false dichotomy between theory and practice).

(c) the lack of consensus about the nature and aims of democratic government (e.g. the dominant emphasis on representative forms and the relative neglect of the participatory perspective).

A whole range of pedagogic questions including the problem of overloading in the curriculum, the existence of 'undemocratic' schools and classrooms which militate against the effectiveness of political education, the problems of teaching technique and the inadequacy of teaching materials, the problem of bias, the absence of appropriately trained teachers, and the inadequacy of existing research will be considered together in Chapter 6. The barriers arising from more fundamental divisions in society are discussed in Chapter 7.

In this chapter attention is mainly directed to the barriers which stem from traditional attitudes and professional hostility to the development of political education. It is not suggested that all of the resistance to this development is at the level of conscious and overt hostility for it is clear that the process of 'accommodating' political literacy objectives sometimes works at an unconscious level especially when these are interpreted in the light of existing frameworks of reference whether radical or conservative. A more conscious concern to 'accommodate' the new development is apparent when it is argued that the political literacy objectives are either met within traditional school subjects or can be readily absorbed within them. Examples will be given of a variety of counter-proposals which, if implemented, would have the effect of modifying, distorting or nullifying the political literacy objectives. It will be seen that the common thread within this particular group of barriers is that of reaction to what is perceived as a challenge to existing vested interests.

Traditional attitudes and professional hostility

The oft-repeated injunction to 'keep politics out of the school', which echoes through school staffrooms and provides familiar headlines in popular newspapers, was uttered with added force when a new form of political education was proposed. The individuals concerned here either do not see that politics is a natural and inescapable part of democratic life or they prefer to ignore this fact in pursuit of their own prejudiced purposes. Whenever someone utters the plea that this or that issue should be 'taken out of politics' (e.g. the retention of grammar schools or independent schools), what he or she really means is that no action should be taken which is prejudicial to his or her own highly political point of view. 'Keeping politics out of school' in reality expresses the conviction that the existing situation, in which the 'hidden curriculum' encourages either passive acceptance of the *status quo* or regrettable withdrawal strategies, should be maintained. The sociological reality is well expressed in a recent book by Maurice Kogan who has no doubt that

education is political. It strongly reflects the often conflicting and wide-ranging preferences of a society which it also helps to sustain, improve, embellish and from which it draws its resources. If politics are the way in which individuals assert their claim and have them reconciled with the claims of others, education reflects and clarifies and expresses those claims in the society, though it cannot of itself reconcile them. (Kogan, 1978, p. 20.)

One of the first and most formidable barriers to the implementation of a programme designed to enhance political literacy is the continuing prevalence of conservative attitudes. Thus, Rhodes Boyson, a former comprehensive-school headmaster and now a Conservative MP and Junior Minister in the Department of Education and Science, reacted to the preliminary announcement of the Hansard Society proposals in an article in *The Times* entitled 'There is More to Life than Learning about Politics'. The article is largely a reiteration of the traditional viewpoint and some might regard it as a classic expression of reactionary prejudice. The following quotations illustrate the view and fears which were then expressed:

If political education is to be introduced into schools, then it should be introduced as a body of knowledge and should cover how local government works, how Parliament works, how the law courts work, the rule of law and the function of the police.

I fear, however, that many children find 'civics' the dullest subject. To come alive the facts have to be embellished and this is where there could be a danger of indoctrination.

As a people we would expect democracy to be shown as preferable to dictatorship and the ballot box as better than the street riot, and the Queen respected as the unifying factor in the Constitution...Is a Soviet regime which has killed or starved to death 66,000,000 of its people to be compared impartially with a liberal democracy? That would certainly be a strange form of political education to introduce into our schools. (Boyson, 1978.)

The article contains some dubious assumptions and proceeds on a form of logic which is not easy to follow. We are told that, if we are to have political education, it *should* be introduced as a body of knowledge of a particular kind. The writer then condemns his own selection and emphasis as being conducive to dullness and suggests that it can *only* be enlivened by embellishment which admits the possibility, and by implication the likelihood, of bias. No one connected with the Programme of Political Education wishes to deny democratic values or to preach the virtues of Soviet Communism. The procedural values advanced by the Programme have been entirely ignored by Mr Boyson. With every allowance for the problems of compression in a newspaper article and due regard for journalistic licence, this seems to be an unfortunate way for an MP and a former headmaster to treat a serious educational argument. One can only hope that experience of ministerial office will produce a change of heart and convince him of the necessity of improving levels of political awareness.

The role of head teachers

In all educational innovations head teachers occupy a key role. It is generally they who guarantee (or fail to guarantee) the degree of institutional support, in terms of the status of the activity, staffing, resources, etc., which are necessary to facilitate the work of the teacher. But head teachers, by and large, are conservatively-minded individuals and this produces considerable difficulties in the kind of development which is envisaged here. In their contribution to the 'Great Debate' on the Government's Green Paper, *Education in Schools*, 1977, a submission from the National Association of Head Teachers urged that 'due attention should be paid to the study of aesthetic and cultural values no less than those which provide the knowlege and skill necessary for the pupil's future life as a political and economic member of the community' (Crick and Porter, 1978, p. 8). Only a few months later the the HMIs' discussion paper (Hennessy and Slater, 1977) was debated at a conference of the Association and this was vigorously attacked by Mr Peter Eckersley, a member of the Association's national council (see the *Guardian*, 31 May 1978). Mr Eckersley accused the HMIs of advocating that controversial issues be considered in school on political rather than traditional ethnical grounds; this, he said, was 'an approach more suited to a Rent-a-mob lecturer'. According to the newspaper report he also considered that 'schools had to find ways of coping with the tiny minority of teachers who regarded things like closed shops and strikes as justifiable because the teachers themselves belong to groups which sought to destroy our society'. To those who have read the HMIs' paper, which is notable for its moderation and restraint, this might seem to be a somewhat prejudiced response; but the conference, which purports to represent 21,000 head teachers, overwhelmingly carried a resolution urging 'caution in accepting recent recommendations that political education should take place in schools' (*Guardian*, 31 May 1978). There is clearly, in the minds of many teachers and head teachers, a great deal of misunderstanding and prejudice on the issue of political education.

As J. Webb (1962) and others have shown, the school itself is a powerful agent in professional socialisation which tends strongly towards conservatism in educational thought and practice. Olive Banks submits that the socialisation of teachers within the school 'will include the transfer not only of official values and objectives but informal goals, ideologies and procedures' (Banks, 1968, p. 198). It is for this reason that the maximum degree of support for the development of political literacy as a legitimate and necessary feature of educational endeavour should be given by the Department of Education and Science and local education authorities. A number of short courses and conferences held during 1978–9 which were in part supported by DES funds have led to a softening of these attitudes in the areas where they have been held. This is especially true in the few cases where Directors of Educational Services and representatives of the LEA advisory staffs have attended the conferences and made clear their sympathy and support for the aims of political education (see Chapter 4).

Accommodation processes

A further problem arises even when there is genuine sympathy with a proposed educational innovation because of the tendency, which exists in all of us, to interpret and qualify a new information and events in terms of our own existing frameworks of reference. In some ways this is harder to overcome than outright opposition to a new development because there is always the danger that agreement will be reached on the necessity for change but when the change is implemented it may be carried out in a manner which will distort or destroy its intentions. This may be referred to as the process of accommodation.

Thus, in November 1977, Norman St John Stevas, MP, the then Conservative Opposition spokesman on Education, apparently became persuaded that the kind of approach being developed by the Hansard Society Working Party was worthy of support and addressed the Birmingham Bow Group on the theme of 'Political Education in Schools'. He said: 'We face a double danger: either it (political education) will atrophy and die or it will be exploited by those who wish to misuse it for their own totalitarian ends. There is a *via media* or a third way out of this dilemma, and that is to build up a consensus among the democratic political parties on the approach to the problem.' So far, so good; but the following extracts illustrate the way in which the proposals were in fact interpreted in a way which blunted their cutting edge and, one presumes unintentionally, distorted their true purpose:

But the course of instruction to be followed should be factual and objective and dispassionately presented. There are some values on which neutrality is not enough. We may legitimately expect from those teaching in our schools commitment to the Crown and the Constitution. Loyalty to the monarch and our traditional liberties are not optional extras but an intrinsic part of the value system which we may legitimately expect to be transmitted through our maintained school system.

A basic explanation of the relationship between our political system and our economic system would be useful – the belief in a mixed economy as a means of combining help for the weak with the safeguarding of freedom. (St John Stevas, 1977.)

The way in which these suggestions in part coincide with the recommendations on developing political literacy but in part distort them is obvious and need not be elaborated here. One is torn between welcome for the clearly expressed desire for consensus and rejection of the unfortunate way in which agreed values are combined with a perhaps unconscious but recognisably partisan viewpoint.

In 1975, Sir Keith Joseph, MP, accepted an invitation to address the annual conference of the Politics Association. With characteristic thoroughness he studied the then draft papers of the Programme for Political Education (the revised editions of which now form Part 2 of Crick and Porter, 1978) and, in his address to the conference, gave a considered comment on them. Sir Keith stated that he was 'very impressed' by 'the efforts to define a framework of explanation that pays fulls respect to tolerance, truth, reason and civilised values' and acknowledged 'the honourable search by partial men for impartiality' (Joseph, 1976, p. 1). He did, however, submit a number of criticisms and make a number of suggestions for extending the range of studies to be incorporated in political syllabuses. Much that he suggested, e.g. on the nature of decision-making and the necessity for an acquaintance with the concepts of Economics, might well assist in the enhancement of political literacy, but others seem to urge an uncritical defence of the basis of the existing economic structure as something inherently desirable and this manifestly detracts from the objectives of political literacy as previously outlined. He recommended an examination of the function of profit and said: 'Profit earned in competition is crucial as a concept to the efficient deployment of resources in a market system...Profit is the main signalling system of a market economy and a free society.' (Joseph, 1976, p. 8.)

Certainly, knowledge of the function and operation of the profit principle is part of political and economic literacy but it would surely be necessary to go beyond this in order to achieve balance by making it clear that not all economic systems depend exclusively on the profit motive. Professor Crick, in his paper on 'Procedural Values in Political Education', refers to Sir Keith's contribution but rejects 'market values' as being 'too partial to be the basis of any possible genuine political education', although they may be considered as part of the subject matter which should be studied as 'doctrines'. Professor Crick writes: 'We deal with conflicts of values. So we protest against any attempts, Marxist or liberal–capitalist, to build into the whole activity of political education the very assumptions that they wish through practice to universalise.' (Crick and Porter, 1978, pp. 64–5.)

In Chapter 6 it will be argued that political and economic literacy go hand in hand and that both should find their place in a common-core curriculum as part of course designed to provide young people with an awareness of 'Man in Society' but since the issue arises here it will be helpful to pursue it a little further. In fact, the approach to the curriculum of secondary schools recently taken by the Economics Association in pursuance of their own particular interest, although arrived at independently, has much in common with that of the Programme for Political Education. A report published in December 1977, observed that 'it should be a major educational objective to ensure that pupils do not leave school wholly ignorant of the economic facts of life and incapable of exercising the powers of discrimination which are necessary in their role as consumers, producers and citizens' (Economics Association, 1977, p. 6). This professional association sees three over-riding purposes for which some education in economics is essential for all pupils of secondary-school age. These are:

(i)   to provide school leavers, within their varying intellectual capacities, with that economic knowledge and those economic skills and concepts which will enable them to better understand the world in which they live, and the sophisticated workings of their own economy.

(ii) to develop an understanding of the more important economic forces and institutions with which they will come into contact as producers and consumers, and of the crucial interdependence of economic actions.

(iii) to ensure that all pupils acquire sufficient knowledge of economics and the methods of the social sciences to enable them to participate fully in the decision-making processes of modern industrial democracy. (Economics Association, 1977, p. 4.)

A rather different form of the 'accommodation process' arises in suggestions that the more traditional subjects in the curriculum either at present adequately incorporate the political dimension or, should it be regarded as necessary, could without undue difficulty accommodate its objectives. Thus, History is frequently seen as a possible and desirable vehicle for carrying political eduction, a claim which has been advanced by school historians and is enshrined in Ministry of Education pamphlets on the teaching of History (see Ministry of Education, 1952 and Department of Education and Science, 1967). The pamphlet *Towards World History* for example, claims that 'most teachers tend to stress the preliminary training which the subject provides in responsible citizenship' and observes that it will be as well to give the rising generation 'as good a political education as may be, which means giving it an education in history' (Department of Education and Science, 1967, p. 2). This claim has been strongly challenged both by historians and others who have demonstrated its invalidity. Ian Lister has stated: 'Perhaps the most common objection to the introduction of political education is the claim that an adequate political education is already gained through such subjects as history... This claim, which has been accepted by too many for too long, needs to be challenged.' (Lister, 1969; see also Burston, 1948 and 1962; Lawton, 1968.)

Derek Heater is a historian who is one of the foremost champions of political education but he recognises the limitations of history as a general vehicle for education in politics. He writes: 'There is no necessary transfer of understanding from the political past to the political present. The civic education function of History can only be performed by studying the past in such a way as to illuminate the present... The function of History is to understand the past, not the present.' (Crick and Heater, 1977, pp. 153–4.)

The objects to the false claim of the 'incidental' approach to political education have been well expressed by Harold Entwistle. He points out that

the problem of teaching anything incidentally is that appropriately illustrative incidents may occur too rarely for the necessary conceptual development to be fostered systematically and adequately. Proper understanding and mastery of facts, concepts and principles requires that these be encountered repeatedly at intervals and in different sorts of contexts. For, in an educational context, 'incidental' has a habit of meaning 'haphazard', and there is no more reason why a child's political education should be left to chance than should his mathematical education... (Entwistle, 1971, p. 108.)

The difficulties of infusing political literacy indirectly were referred to in the Hansard Society report which recognises that the difficulties apply not only to History but even to the conventional GCE A-level courses in British Constitution whose objectives are different to those of the political literacy programme. The report states: 'If the two sets of objectives conflict, it will always be the political literacy objectives that suffer. Partly this is a subject restraint, but (it is) also an examination restraint.' It goes on 'despite obvious advantages,

History and British Government as vehicles for political literacy showed some signs of, at the worst, crushing the hitch-hiker beyond recognition or, at best, of simply taking him somewhere else, certainly compared to even a few hours journey in a vehicle, however small, deliberately set aside for courses designed to enhance political literacy' (Crick and Porter, 1978, p. 24). Although the report posits the possibility of developing political literacy through subjects such as History or English, it is obvious that the 'hitch-hiker principle' must be pursued with great caution because it could all too easily result in an inadequate or fictitious implementation of the objectives of political literacy. The researchers at the University of York end of the Programme for Political Education saw this type of approach, at most, as second best. They say: 'our experience...does not make us optimistic about such approaches. From our research, we concluded that political literacy needs both explicit attention and clear identity.' (Lister, 1977b, p. 111.)

Displacement and dilution

Whenever a new curriculum proposal, more or less specific in its objectives, is mooted, reactions from individual groups with different or complementary educational interests will vary. Some will welcome and support the initiative, others, in pursuit of their own objectives, will either simply oppose it or seek with varying degrees of severity to displace or dilute it. Both of the latter reactions can be observed in relation to the recent proposals for the development of political education.

In September 1977, an all-party group of MPs with an interest in youth organisations became extremely concerned about what they perceived to be the growing problem of political alienation among young people. As a result of parliamentary pressure from this group the Department of Education and Science was persuaded to make a grant to the British Youth Council for the development of political education within its affiliated organisations (see Chapter 4). When this was announced in April 1978, Dr Mia Kellmer Pringle, Director of the National Children's Bureau, who had apparently received a negative response from the Government on proposals to expand facilities for preparing young people for parenthood, argued that this money would be better spent in aiding her own organisation. She is reported (*Guardian*, 22 April 1978) as stating that: 'The vast majority of young people are not going into politics. What you can be sure of is that the vast majority of young people will go on to have children.' One can appreciate and admire the work done by Dr Kellmer Pringle and the National Children's Bureau and might well wish that this was better funded than it apparently is. It is a pity, however, that she should seek to deprecate the provision of such a modest sum for the development of political education among young people in order to pursue her own worthy cause. The purpose of the political education project is sadly misrepresented and to argue at this level is to do less than justice to the case for the development of political education *or* education for parenthood.

The publication of the HMIs' discussion paper on 'Political Competence' in *The Times Educational Supplement* on 25 November 1977 (referred to above, pp. 52–3) gave rise to a number of pleas which illustrate the way in which organisations with interests cognate to those of the Hansard Society Programme for Political Education accepted the move towards political education, but then attempted to qualify or widen it to accommodate their own particular concerns. Thus, the late John Sewell, who was then Chairman of The European–Atlantic Movement (TEAM), felt that the HMIs' document failed to take account of the fact that 'politics does not stop at Dover' and that mention should be made of 'the need to acquaint the oncoming generation of the problems faced by détente, deterrence and defence...'; he argued for a renewed emphasis upon the 'ancient values' which underlie the democracies of Western Europe and North America as a defence against 'other ideologies' which 'do not "discuss" them with balanced pros and cons...' (*The Times Educational Supplement*, 9 December 1977). This avowedly partisan approach clearly runs counter to the spirit of the recommendations made by the two HMIs and the Hansard Society Working Party recommendations which to a large extent their article reflects.

The need for a clear-cut national policy on political education, founded on something like the objectives of the political literacy approach, became even clearer two years later when it became apparent that The European–Atlantic Movement, which was said to have received funds from the Foreign Office and the US Government, had arranged for a project designed in accordance with its objectives of 'enlarging public awareness of the European and Atlantic Communities'. In the evolution of the project its title was changed from 'Democracy, Détente, Deterrence and Defence' to 'Towards Political Competence in an Open Society', a change which presumably reflected a desire to legitimise the activity of this group by bringing it into line with the terminology of the HMIs' document on 'Political Competence'. When the details were announced in the *Guardian* on 21 June 1979, Frank Allaun, MP, urged that the project should be immediately abandoned. In an article in the *New Statesman* (6 July 1979), Rick Rogers asserted that: TEAM's work appears to be directly linked to NATO's own research programme. For this includes a project on the image of NATO in the public sector of secondary education in England.' He asks, why should help and facilities be given 'to an insignificant and questionable organisation such as TEAM well out of the mainstream of curriculum research and development and at the same time by-passing more able and experienced bodies in the process'. As far as the present writer has been able to trace, no official response has come from the Department of Education and Science but this is clearly a matter which raises a basic question on the role of political education in schools, and it would be interesting to know the official reason for the apparently favourable financial treatment which TEAM has received.

In the same edition of *The Times Educational Supplement* in which the TEAM case was briefly made, Chris Brown, the then Chairman of the Association for the Teaching of Social Science, regretted the specific emphasis on the political dimension. He stated:

Something more than political education is called for... The social world is too complex for it to be understood through one subject area. A whole range of social science and humanities subjects must be used to create a curriculum which will reflect the nature of today's world. Most of these are already in the schools, so that the main problem is to develop and improve existing courses such as social studies, rather than to introduce new ones.

This response appeared to strike a heavily discordant note and it is unfortunately the case that in the earlier phases of the development of the two associations a degree of misunderstanding and mutual suspicion was discernible. This was especially apparent in relation to the Association for the Teaching of Social Science's interest in political education and there was, on the part of some members of the Politics Association, a feeling that what they believed to be a necessary and specific emphasis on political education was in danger of being lost sight of within the wider view of social-science teaching adopted by the Association for the Teaching of Social Science.

In fact, some of the prominent figures in the Politics Association shared the conviction of the Association for the Teaching of Social Science that political education should form part of a broader scheme for the study of society in schools underpinned by the perspectives and methods of the social sciences. This view was, however, usually qualified by an insistence on having a clearly defined place for political education within such a wider course. Thus, the Report of the Political Education Research Unit of the University of York stated that courses in political education 'should not be isolated under such headings as "Politics", "Civics", or "The Constitution" but should be part of a more comprehensive Social Studies programme'. It added: 'However political education should not merge into the general programme to the extent that it loses its identity – in the minds of the students, if not the teachers.' (Lister, 1977b, p. 111.) The Hansard Society report observed: 'Social studies has an internal tension between those who see it as something very specific (usually schools of sociology) and therefore, in theory at least, very open to inter-disciplinary co-operation, and those who see it as very wide, a comprehensive social science, so wide indeed that like the jaws of the Lady of Riga's tiger, it tends to swallow rather than relate to those subjects like economics and politics, which it regards as its own sub-categories.' (Crick and Porter, 1978, p. 23.)

Happily, in recent months, a very close co-operation between the three associations concerned with social, economic and political education, viz: the Association for the Teaching of Social Science, the Economics Association and the Politics Association, has developed. Following meetings between the officers of the three associations, joint working parties have been established to look at both curriculum concerns and organisational matters. The Curriculum Working Party, on which the three chairmen sit, intends to prepare a statement of 'the aims and general objectives of social, political and economic education with reference to the 14–16 age group' and the other group is examining 'the possibilities for increased co-operation between the Associations to the mutual benefit of their members in the short, medium, and long term'.

This is a constructive and positive development because professional associations with complementary or overlapping interests have little to gain and much to lose if they allow themselves to engage in organisational in-fighting merely to preserve or extend their own particular objectives. On the other hand it must be recognised that these specialist professional associations represent legitimate and important special interests and it is perfectly reasonable that they should seek to ensure that these interests are reflected in the school curriculum. Protagonists of a new form of political education should be among the first to recognise that politics is not the whole of life, but a large part of their case is that it is an important part of life which has not, so far, been adequately represented in the schools. There is always the danger that its role and function could be obscured, diminished or negated unless it retains its identify as a necessary ingredient in the curriculum, although being studied along with other facets of society which may require different perspectives and methodologies.

In this chapter attention has been drawn to what are judged to be some very real barriers to the development of political education. If political literacy programmes are to be introduced into the schools these will, in one way or another, have to be overcome. Some encouragement can be drawn from the fact that the problems and possibilities inherent in the proposed changes are now being openly discussed and the need for a realistic programme for political education suited to a modern industrial democracy is at least formally recognised by the Department of Education and Science, and that active efforts towards this end are being made by a number of local education authorities as well as by an increasing number of individual teachers. The implications of this development need to be further examined and more widely discussed. Ideally, this discussion would included not only politicians and teachers but also representatives of the wider public, perhaps through the involvement of governing bodies of schools, parents' associations, community groups and a wide range of voluntary organisations.

But aims and objectives, however enlightened and worthy, must be translated into viable educational programmes and this is no minor undertaking. Some of the more pressing organisational and pedagogic implications are examined in the next chapter.

6 Teachers and schools

'Educators should know they are political beings. When they unveil social reality they have problems.'

Paulo Freire, *in conversation with Ian Lister* (1973b)

'A politically literate adult population produced by a systematic programme of political education in our schools and colleges is the best guarantee against the indoctrinator. Fear of indoctrination should not be a barrier to political education but rather a stimulus to its introduction and development.'

Jonathan F. Brown (1975)

Political education and the curriculum

Any examination of the barriers to the introduction and development of political education must include some consideration of a number of problems including those connected with school organisation, teaching styles and methods, teacher training, resources and research. If the need for a new form of political education is conceded, one of the first problems is to find a place for it in a curriculum which is already grossly overcrowded. In staking its claim for inclusion political education jostles with education for parenthood, the understanding of industry, education for leisure, and other worthy causes, all of which are being pressed upon the school as being vital as a preparation for adult life in a modern industrial society.

It is not proposed to embark here upon a detailed examination of the curriculum and on assessment of the merits of the many competing claims upon the time and resources of school. The problem of the overcrowded curriculum is a real one and this situation, not infrequently, is used as an excuse to resist the inclusion of desirable elements within it. The obvious solution would seem to lie in the adoption of a common-core curriculum with a substantial time allocation to be taken by all pupils. This would be accompanied by a programme of optional studies from which the individual could choose in accordance with his or her personal interests and intended career. The essential argument for the common-core curriculum is that all pupils should have the opportunity of reaching a minimum level of understanding and experience in these areas of the curriculum which are regarded as being of central importance in the development of the human personality and preparation for life in a complex society. This would, it is hoped, also serve to ensure at least a token compliance with the ideal of equality of opportunity in education. Beyond the core curriculum there should be available a series of options, including political studies, some of which would give opportunities of more specialised studies in the elements of the common core while others might open up new areas of knowledge or fields of interest.

The way in which such an arrangement could be organised has been convincingly argued by Denis Lawton (1973 and 1975) in his plea for the establishment of a 'common culture curriculum'. In *Social Change, Educational Theory and Curriculum Planning*, he writes: 'We have to begin with the recognition that the organisation of many schools is less rational than it could be and involves a great deal more wasted time than now can be afforded. But simply to add more subjects to the timetable is untidy and unnecessary.' (Lawton, 1973, p. 139.) Some possible formulations of the core curriculum were based on Hirst's 'forms of knowledge' (Hirst and Peters, 1970) or some similar schematic presentation: other candidates for consideration, which are summarised in *Class, Culture and the Curriculum* (Lawton, 1975) include the schemes of Broudy (1962), Peterson (1960), Phenix (1964) and Williams (1961). It is worth noticing, in passing, that it has been the exception rather than the rule for such categorisations of knowledge or curriculum construction to identify the political dimension of human experience. The most specific inclusion of a political component in such schemes is that detailed in Raymond Williams's plan for a reformed curriculum which is based upon a historical analysis of our culture. This includes 'social history, law and political institutions, sociology, descriptive economics...taught not as disciplines but as general knowledge drawn from the disciplines', together with 'extensive practice in democratic procedures, including meetings, negotiations, and the selection and conduct of leaders in democratic organisation. Extensive practice in the use of libraries, newspapers and magazines, radio and television programmes, and other sources of information, opinion and influence.' (Williams, 1961, pp. 174–5.)

Lawton's core curriculum is based on 'disciplines' not 'subjects' as traditionally taught in grammar schools and he points out that 'a curriculum based on disciplines does not rule out the possibility of interdisciplinary work', nor does it prevent the work done being 'related to the children's own experience and interests' (Lawton, 1975, pp. 84–5). This curriculum will be guided by the principles of 'coverage' and 'balance', i.e. 'Nothing important should be missed out from our selection... but also everything should be included in a considered proportion.' The important decisions on what is to be included and what is to be excluded proceed by a process of 'infusion together with integration'. If, therefore, neglected subjects are not just tacked on but incorporated within the bodies of knowledge being deemed most appropriate with the unnessary and unhelpful elements being, presumably, ruthlessly excised. Lawton sets out clearly the stages by which the necessary task of planning the actual curriculum should proceed:

Stage 1. Seeks answers to fundamental questions about aims, what is deemed worthwhile, the structure of knowledge and how these ideas interact with societal considerations.

Stage 2. Takes into account the nature of modern society, how and why it developed in that way, social changes (technological and ideological) which influence education, the needs of the individual in society.

Stage 3. Makes the *ideal* selection from culture taking into account the interplay of answers from Stages 1 and 2.

Stage 4. Brings into operation such an assessment of psychological theories such as Piaget's work on the stages of development and Bruner's idea on a 'theory of instruction' in order to ensure that what is contemplated is reasonably within the realm of pedagogic possibility.

Stage 5. Plans a more detailed curriculum (in the light of the earlier considerations) setting out the approach to the work to be undertaken in terms of stages, sequences etc.

State 6. Examines necessary modifications, taking into account practical limitations on staffing and resources.

Stage 7. Translates what is possible into a workable timetable.

As Lawton points out, it will also be necessary to monitor the development of the teaching programme in an effort to ensure that the curriculum is actually achieving what is sets out to do (Lawton, 1973, ch. 1). If something like this procedure were to be followed in curriculum planning it would go a long way towards the more systematic formulation of answers to the four fundamental questions which Ralph Tyler thought must be asked in relation to any curriculum. These were:

(i)   What educational purposes should the school seek to attain?

(ii) What educational experiences can be provided that are likely to attain these purposes?
(iii) How can these educational experiences be effectively organised?
(iv) How can we determined whether these purposes are being attained? (R. Tyler, 1949, quoted in Lawton, 1973, p. 13.)

Lawton's proposals for a comprehensive review of the curriculum are important because they provide the only real answer to a reform of the curriculum which will enable the dead wood to be cut away and a new, more vigorous tree to be grown.

As mentioned in Chapter 4, recent thinking within the Department of Education and Science, and especially among HMIs, has moved firmly in the direction of a core curriculum for all pupils in the secondary school. Their view of the curriculum is an inclusive one. In *A View of the Curriculum*, it is suggested that:

The curriculum in its full sense comprises all the opportunities for learning provided by the school. It included the formal programme of lessons in the time-table; the so-called 'extra-curricular' and 'out of school' activities deliberately promoted or supported by the school; and the climate of relationships, attitudes, styles of behaviour and the general quality of life established in the school community as a whole. (Department of Education and Science, 1980a, p. 2.)

The Curriculum 11–16: Working Papers by H.M. Inspectors also makes clear that the importance of the 'hidden curriculum' has been clearly recognised. It is accepted that 'curricula give out messages' and that 'in any curriculum the selection of subjects and skills to be taught and the attitudes and activities that are encouraged implies certain political and social assumptions and values, however un-conscious' (Department of Education and Science, 1979a, p. 10).

The same document follows Lawton and others in seeing the curriculum as a 'selection from culture' and views pupils in schools as the inheritors of a complex culture with 'a right to be introduced to a selection from its essential elements' (p. 5). It believes that this right can best be realised in the school through the introduction of a common-core curriculum which comprises 'perhaps as much as two-third or three-quarters of the time available' (p. 6). The 'selection from culture' proposed delineates eight essential 'areas of experi-ence', including 'the social and political'. These categories are repeated in the DES Consultative Document, *A Framework for the School Curriculum* (Department of Education and Science, 1980b), in which the Secretaries of State make clear their intention to seek 'a national consensus' on a desirable framework for the school curriculum. As indicated in Chapter 4, this initiative was welcomed by the Politics Association; it was also favourably received by the Association for the Teaching of Social Science and the Economics Association.

The Politics Association accepted that the Secretaries of State 'have an inescapable duty to satisfy themselves that the work of the school matches national needs' (Department of Education and Science, 1980b, p. 1) but urged that this requirement should not be viewed in narrow economic terms. It stressed that the concept of national needs also embraces political and social requirements. The Association rejected the view that social and political objectives do not require the introduction of new subjects into the curriculum and expressed the hope that the essential requirements of the 'social and political' area of experience would not be overlooked in a possible preoccupation with the more traditional areas of the curriculum (see Appendix III).

There is still much resistance to the idea of a common-core curriculum on the part of teachers' associations and individual teachers and head teachers. It would seem, however, that the logic of curriculum development points to such an arrangement as one of the preconditions of curricular reform. Those interested in establishing the claims of social and political education have much to gain by keeping abreast of these wider developments and they should continue to make positive contributions to the ongoing discussion.

Constitutional *v.* political approaches

The nature of the traditional Civics and British Constitution courses, which had much in common, has been referred to earlier. It was observed that the emphasis of these courses was formalistic, procedural and descriptive with political controversies being either avoided or defused. There was thought to be no problem of bias because everything was made 'neutral' and safe in accordance with the prevailing norms of society; the actual bias was conservative and conformist. The major criticisms of the constitutional perspective have been well expressed by Crick:

There are three objections at least to beginning with 'the constitution', and these objections apply to beginning with 'good citizenship'. (i) There is no such thing which is not in itself a matter of intense political dispute. (ii) It is usually a subterfuge to escape *nasty* politics and usually does the very thing it seeks to avoid: insinuate partisan biases, none the less real for being oblique. (iii) It makes an interesting project dull, safe and factual. There is no constitution in the sense that syllabuses usually asume (it is a concept invented to be taught to others), or rather there is one in a highly abstract sense which is difficult to grasp. (Crick, 1969, p. 4.)

The Working Party of the Programme for Political Education took the view that the dullness and aridity of the traditional approach should be replaced by one aiming at the enhancement of 'political literacy' (see pp. 55–7). This involves an attempt to develop conceptual awareness through an examination of real political issues and adherence to approved 'procedural values'. It was hoped that this would provide 'the knowledge, skills and attitudes needed to make a man or woman informed about politics; able to participate in public life and groups of all kinds, both occupational and voluntary; and to recognise and tolerate diversities in social and political values' (see Crick and Porter, 1978, pp. 37–46). Following the close observation of teaching based on these principles, the assessors of the Programme for Political Education, based both in London and York, claimed that the objectives of political literacy are capable of attainment in a wide variety of contexts. Crick and Porter observe: 'The teachers participating in the project have clearly demonstrated that with a minimum of guidance they can translate the theoretical precepts of political literacy into realistic classroom practice.' (Crick and Porter, 1978, p. 17.) The York team concluded that 'courses in political education following the Political Literacy approach, are possible, viable, and can be impressive' (Lister, 1977b, p. 110). These investigators identify the main factors which make for successful teaching in this field and draw attention to drawbacks and deficiencies which inhibit the work as well as commenting on some misplaced fears. Some of the major aspects considered are examined below.

Theories and definitions of politics

It has already been suggested that a theory of political education presupposes a theory of politics (see Chapter 1). The Working Party of the Programme for Political Education was conscious of this fact and based its recommendations on a view of politics as an activity essentially concerned with 'the creative conciliation of differing interests, whether these interest are seen as material or moral' (Crick and Porter, 1978, p. 4.) Theories of politics, whether as a human activity, a discipline of study or both are many and varied (see e.g. Crick, 1964 and 1966; Miller, 1965) but it is clear that such theories, whether in study and teaching, political analysis or participation, lend a sense of direction and purpose to the activity being pursued.

In its assessment of the teaching of politics in schools and further education colleges, the observers from the Political Education Research Unit at the University of York identified three different conceptions of politics which were defined as:

(i)   *The restricted conception* (the politics of state power, major political parties, national political figures).

(ii) *The extended conception* (the politics of institutions such as schools and colleges, firms and factories).

(iii) *The inclusive conception* (the politics of space, the politics of the environment). (Lister, 1977b, p. 58; see also pp. 96–7.)

These categories at once embrace three more or less distinctive possible approaches to the study of politics in schools and, to some extent, the different approaches actually observed. The main emphasis here is on the nature and range of the content but it is evident that such a selection, consciously or unconsciously, has a theoretical basis. The conclusion reached by these observers was that, in the teaching of politics in schools, a clear recognition of the theory of politics on which the teaching is based is of the utmost importance for teacher and pupil alike.

Lister suggests that for a teacher engaged in political education, 'any coherent theory of politics, from the point of view of efficiency and teaching is better than none at all' (Lister, 1977a, p. 4). He reports that some teachers they observed based their lessons on a theory which was not readily apparent and sometimes shifted from one theory to another without explanation or even perhaps without realising that they were doing this. He writes: 'Sometimes too, teachers who has a broad view of politics would, nevertheless, give the impression, even through explicit statements to their pupils that political participation was the same thing as voting in General Elections.' (Lister, 1977b, p. 99.) The distinction made earlier between the conceptions of *representative* democracy and that of *participatory* democracy (see Chapter 1) is relevant here. Voting in a general election is a minimal form of political activity different in kind and degree from an informed and committed involvement in local groups and organisations and constructively critical responses to issues of local, regional and national concern. Lister observes: 'The first can see politically educated people as discriminatory consumers of the political services of others; the second looks not only to central government but also in the workplace, and the politics of everyday life.' (Lister, 1977a, p. 14.)

Such distinctions go beyond mere academic fussiness; they tend towards clarity in discussion and teaching and hence aid the possibilities of successful conceptual development. If a teacher is seeking to enhance political literacy in accordance with the canons laid down in the report he must be conscious of the importance of the theory of politics which he embraces. If the teacher is confused then the pupils are likely to be confused. A clear framework of reference is of considerable educational importance.

Bias – a bogus problem?

Discussion on political education in schools has been bedevilled by the twin bogies of 'indoctrination' and 'bias'. Sometimes the concerned expressed is genuine, in others it appears to be an excuse for opposing the introduction of politics or for professional inactivity. The concern is understandable but unnecessarily exaggerated. The conventional desiderata of 'the teacher's duty' in this respect have been succinctly enumerated by Derek Heater:

In the first place, he must know himself – be honest enough with himself to be aware quite clearly what his position is on the controversial issues he is going to teach. Secondly, he must have enough professional integrity to refrain from the conscious indoctrination of his pupils. Thirdly, his examination must be thorough enough to prevent him from engaging in unconscious indoctrination. in the fourth place, he must have sufficient skill and humility to open his pupils' eyes to all points of view and encourage them to think out their own attitudes. And finally, he must have a relationship with his class that is free enough for them to *want* to think and not be swayed by the teacher's personal opinion. But, above all, the teacher of political subjects must have skill and confidence in handling difficult and complex material. (Heater, 1969a, p. 63.)

This is not to suggest that the teacher must be politically emasculated; it would, indeed, be surprising if the teacher of politics did not have strong convictions on the central questions of political debate. Bias cannot be eliminated but it can be recognised and coped with in politics as in other subjects where, all too frequently, it may be condoned or pass unnoticed. What is being advocated here is that it is the responsibility of the teacher to acknowledge and encourage an awareness of a diversity of viewpoints on important matters and he must try to make those which he does not personally accept at least as plausible as his own.

The problem of bias was recognised and confronted in the investigations of both the London and York research teams. The Hansard Society Report observes: 'While we share the fears of L.E.A.s and parents that there can sometimes be gross bias in the classroom (whatever the subject), we do not share the hopes of those who believe that methodologies can be produced which are guaranteed value-free and will eliminate bias.' (Crick and Porter, 1978, p. 5.) The report makes clear that the answer lies largely in a style of teaching which is truly professional and states:

One should be dispassionate, rational, sensible, in a phrase, professional and responsible, but nothing can guarantee that one can be without bias. To think otherwise is self-deception, and it may not even be a sensible desire. For there is bias and biases. Teachers should be aware of their own biases, and being aware of them, increase their empathy for the plausibility of other biases. While it is right to seek to contain prejudices, it is not always either right or possible to seek to eliminate prejudice. Part of teaching is to make pupils aware of their own biases, the biases of others in the class and outside, and to alert them to the implications of particular prejudice or perspectives. Such bias is human, venal, inevitable and actually educational...Teachers can actually go beyond 'mere bias' into positive indoctrination (whether conscious or unconscious) if something is taught as the truth regardless of the consideration of evidence and if the pupil is not introduced emphathetically to alternative viewpoints and alternative sources of evidence. (Crick and Porter, 1978, pp. 5–6. See also Snook, 1972a and 1972b; Heater, 1969a; Brennan and Brown, 1975; Crick and Heater, 1977.)

This statement has been reproduced at length because of the importance attached by hostile critics of political education to the problems of bias and indoctrination. The Working Party's response on this should also be linked with the importance attached to the 'procedural values' of freedom, toleration, fairness, respect for truth and respect for reasoning; in this connection it is argued that: 'The study of politics cannot be neutral towards these values: its own existence depends on encouraging them, indeed it presupposes their existence.' (Crick and Porter, 1978, p. 16.)

It is clear from the York Report that the teachers observed were very conscious of and sensitive to the possible impact of their own value positions. The researchers, therefore, interviewed students with a view to trying to ascertain the extent to which they were aware of the teacher's personal views. The researchers concluded that the students 'had a clear and accurate view of the value position of the teacher; made allowances for it and did not see it as a problem'. They comment: 'Therefore if political education teachers worry about whether or not they should make their value position explicit to the student,...they are worrying unnecessarily. This particular dilemma seems to us to be a bogus problem.' Although these observers have no recorded instances of students simply following the values of their teachers they take the view that: 'The problems of bias, prejudice and indoctrination need to be taken much further than the present speculative literature, and even further than we have taken them in our own research.' (Lister, 1977b, p. 66 and pp. 101–2.)*

It is worth noting here that in those schools where political education is now taking place there have been few reports of problems arising from allegations of indoctrination or bias in the teaching. It would appear that, to a large extent, to be conscious of the problem is to solve it.

* For a more recent exchange of views on this subject see articles by J. F. Brown, A. Porter and A. P. Dobson in *Teaching Politics*, vol. 9, no. 3.

The teacher – attitudes and methods

Research findings from Scotland and from overseas suggest that great thought and care must be given to the development of political education in schools if it is to be successful in fulfilling its intended objectives. Thus, Howard Mehlinger reported that conventional Civics courses in the USA which, significantly, avoided 'controversial issues' and made 'little or no effort to develop skills of enquiry in a rigorous and systematic way, were unsuccessful in advancing students' understanding about American political values' (Mehlinger, 1967, pp. 13–18). In relation to the Soviet Union, Azreal (1965) observed that 'the reaction of a large percentage of Soviet pupils to political education was indifference and apathy' (quoted in Heater, 1969b, pp. 41–2). Nearer home, Geoffrey Mercer assessed the educational impact of the Scottish Modern Studies programme, which he described as 'the Scottish version of a direct political education course'. From this study he concluded that 'the impact of Modern Studies tends to fluctuate across areas, although it is true to say that at no stage can we support any conclusions which categorises it as a major factor in learning' (Mercer, 1973, p. 13). Mercer was, however, at pains to point out that this did not cast formal political education as a worthless educational exercise and he urged that there should be no generalisation from this to other educational orientations and contexts. In crude terms, there is at least the possibility that better political education may produce better educational results and it is clear that, in a number of ways, those concerned with the development of the political literacy programme have taken this into account.

Thus, the York team point out that the Programme for Political Education put great stress on 'procedural values' which require and encourage certain behavioural dispositions for teachers and taught. They emphasise strongly that these values must be rigidly adhered to by the teacher. They write:

It seems to us that this kind of political education could fully flourish only if given a certain kind of classroom climate (a democratic classroom) and a certain kind of pedagogy, in particular, one in which a teacher can use a wide range of teaching and learning methods in order to actively involve the majority of students, and in which the teacher has mastered a technique of open, directional questioning, in order to encourage the exploration of political issues by all of the students). (Lister, 1977b, p. 102.)

Independently, one of the London observers concludes: 'The style of the teaching and general atmosphere of the school should be versatile, open and reasonably "democratic", that is, enabling considerable student participation in as many aspects of the programme as possible.' He noted that:

This close correlation between student participation and the success of the programme arises not simply because some of the project recommendations depend upon such participation, but also because it seems likely that the teaching and learning of concepts and procedural values in particular is better undertaken in this way than by the formal stance of lecturing...The chances of success increased with more versatile and adaptable teaching language and style. (Crick and Porter, 1978, pp. 202–3.)

All of this underlines the need, in political education, for the extensive use of what Douglas Barnes (Barnes *et al.* 1969) calls 'exploratory' language in order to prevent premature closure of discussion and to ensure that the students' relevant experiences are willingly contributed and utilised in the search for understanding.

As Harold Entwistle (1971) has advocated and as both the London and York teams have recognised, the school itself could be a powerful political educator and the research programme raised the two related questions of 'What is a democratic classroom?' and 'What is a democratic school?' The Hansard Society Working Party states:

Nowhere do we argue against authority in schools: on the contrary, a legitimate authority can allow itself to be questioned, perhaps even thrives on questioning. Political literacy need not begin with discussing the school itself as a system of political authority: but it may be the mark of a 'good school' that this can be done without fear. (Crick and Porter, 1978, p. 28.)

Schools are traditionally authoritarian and hierarchical structures which have responded but slowly to outside pressure, but changes are taking place, nonetheless, and it would be exceedingly useful and informative, as the York Report suggests, if research could be undertaken on classroom climates and institutional atmospheres to try to discover the appropriate settings for genuinely democratic leadership and participation. As observed in Chapter 4, the researches of Gabriel Almond and Sidney Verba (1963) have made it abundantly clear that young people who have experience of participation in decision-making at home and in school are much more likely than others to believe that they can influence the decisions of government.

Michael Rutter's recent study of secondary schools and their effects on pupils is suggestive in this connection. The conclusion is that the ethos of the school is of vital importance. He and his colleagues found that pupil behaviour, attendance, attainment and deliquency 'were systematically and strongly associated with the characteristics of schools as social institutions' (Rutter *et al.*, 1979, p. 205). Rutter observes that 'one of the consistent findings of other research is that shared activities towards a common goal which requires people to work together are a most effective means of reducing intergroup conflict'. He goes on: 'Mere contact in pleasant surroundings does little to reduce conflict; single episodes of co-operation have little effect; and verbal agreements on goals are not much help. Rather, it is *joint* working together over time for the same purpose which helps to break down barriers.' (p. 196.)

If schools are genuinely concerned to prepare future citizens for life in a democratic society then it is surely time that the educational possibilities inherent in their own structure and organisation are opened to scrutiny with a view to examining what reasonable changes might be made towards this end.

Barriers to curriculum innovation

Considerable difficulties are presented in the implementation of educational changes, especially when they are in such a sensitive area as political education. Neal Gross and his colleagues have suggested that the commonly-held assumption that teachers are resistant to change needs to be challenged and contended that, in many organisations, 'the empirical reality is that a number of their members are exposed to irritating problems and needless strain, and consequently welcome innovations that appear to offer solutions to their difficulties' (Gross *et al.*, 1971, p. 204).

These investigators, however, recognised that the acceptance of the need for change and willingness to undertake it are not, of themselves, enough to ensure the successful implementation of the change proposed. In their own study of curriculum innovation they identified a number of barriers to change which included:

(i)   lack of clarity about the new role model
(ii) lack of knowledge and skills to carry it out
(iii) lack of materials and equipment
(iv) the existence of organisational arrangements incompatible with the innovation. (Gross *et al.*, 1971, pp. 196–8.)

They, therefore, urged the necessary provision for these barriers to be overcome and suggested 'the importance of the need for a strategy for effective feedback between the initiators of the change and those who must implement it, and which maintains efficient problem-solving mechanisms for both unanticipated and anticipated issues which arise during the period of attempted innovation' (p. 215).

These are considerations which apply in political education as well as other aspects of curriculum development. Attention has already been drawn to the need for a form of school organisation and teaching styles which are appropriate to the task of achieving political literacy objectives and in the sections which follow consideration is given to some of the deficiencies in resources and teacher training which will have to be remedied before programmes of political education can be developed on a wide scale.

Resources

Both the Hansard Society Report and the York Report make references to the inadequacy of resources as regards the quantity and types available. Detailed studies need to be made of method and materials for political education and this is unlikely to result from the enthusiasm of activists alone, however valuable this may be. The fact is that much of the existing material on politics for schools was designed for British Constitution and Civics oriented courses and is unsuitable for use in achieving the objectives of political literacy. In 1973–4, the present writer surveyed a wide range of teaching materials for the teaching of politics in schools including works reference, textbooks, workbooks, topic books and audio-visual aids. It was found that GCE A-level and O-level courses are reasonably well provided for and some promising written material for CSE and General Studies courses was beginning to appear. Audio-visual materials, however, were depressingly deficient and books and other resources suitably appropriate to what came to be the 'political literacy' objectives were virtually non-existent (Brennan, 1974, ch. 3; see also author's review of introductory texts in *Parliamentary Affairs*, Autumn 1976, 1977, 1978 and 1979). If attempts are to be made to arouse the interest of young people through an examination of regional and local issues the problem is even further accentuated.

It was not the purpose of the Programme for Political Education to provide materials but the difficulties of trying to realise its objectives without suitable materials quickly became apparent. The only specific recommendation made by the London-based group (and this is probably the weakest section of its report) is that there should be trials of 'some kind of low-cost weekly or fortnightly magazines for schools which contain topical documentation drawn from the Press, parties and pressure groups' (Crick and Porter, 1978, p. 29). The York-based group recommended that more work should be done to identify and establish the content of political literacy courses and to provide suitable teaching materials. They suggested that 'this content would be defined in terms of exemplary political issues and appropriate skills for handling them', and concluded: 'Guidelines (similar to the *Richtlinien* for political education of such West German *Länder* as Hessen and Nordrhein-Westfalen), for content and should be drawn up by an appropriate group, including Her Majesty's Inspectors, professional associations, teachers and research workers.' (Lister, 1977b, p. 110.) The York Report also recognised that 'other agencies and people must recognise *their* responsibilities for improved political education. These include the newspapers, television, industry and trade unions, and political leaders themselves.' (p. 114.)

Policy recommendations on these wider considerations were beyond the scope of the Hansard Society research programme but a few comments might usefully be made here. A variety of pressure groups including for example the Trades Union Congress and Shelter have, albeit on a small scale, produced material designed for use in schools. The difficulty is that this material is prepared not in order to enhance political literacy but in an attempt to gain the sympathy of young people for their own particular points of view. In the hands of a skilled teacher such material can be appropriately edited and handled but this degree of expertise cannot be taken for granted. If organisations such as the CBI and TUC are serious about the comments made on political education in the 'Great Debate' (see Chapter 4) then it is perhaps not too much to hope that they could, through their own respective education departments, be persuaded to co-operate in this endeavour. If a lead of this kind were to be given other organisations, including political parties, government departments and local authorities might, in due course, be persuaded to follow.

In the late 1970s, John Sutton, as Chairman of the Politics Association, prepared a paper entitled 'Parliament, the Public and Political Education' which was submitted to the House of Commons Committee on Services, to which Mr Sutton was subsequently called to give evidence. In this paper suggestions were made on the conduct of visits to the House by young people and it expressed the view that the task of explaining the work of Parliament should be placed in the hands of trained teachers – a practice that was long ago adopted by some museums! It was also recommended that a general public and education service should be set up which would:

(i) provide a general information service, backed up by appropriate publications,
(ii) answer public queries,
(iii) produce summaries of important parliamentary papers, including summaries of key debates,
(iv) produce materials on Parliament suitable for educational use. (Sutton, 1977, p. 27.)

Some of these recommendations were acted upon and an education officer was appointed in the autumn of 1979. A useful start has been made in the pursuit of the objectives listed but one has the impression, however, that the relatively junior status of the education officer, the absence of supporting staff and her limited access to Members, place appreciable limitations on the prospect of further developments in this area.

The role of television

Since most young people obtain a large proportion of their political information from television and some 20 million people watch the main television news bulletins each night it is reasonable to suggest that, among the outside agencies, the BBC and the independent television companies have a special responsibility in relation to political education. The general public sees the presentation of political news and current affairs on television as impartial but this is not the view of political parties, trade unions and some academic investigators. Television selects and defines the issues presented and treats them in the light of its own particular perspectives and criteria. A frequent complaint is that political matters are 'personalised' and 'trivialised', i.e. issues are presented in terms of disputes between leading political personalities instead of the underlying differences and complex political problems are grossly oversimplified.

Sometimes there is a continuing emphasis on a particular issue or problem selected for attention but little effort is made to extend and refine the levels of understanding. Jay Blumler states:

Nothing is so depressing... as the repetitive frequency with which the mass media tend to hammer single-mindedly at some favoured aspect of a question which has aroused public concern, without seizing the opportunity created by such concern to extend the average man's frontiers of awareness, to question some of his more simple assumptions and to render more complex some of his stereotyped impressions of the chief forces at work in a situation.' (Blumer, 1974, pp. 97–8.)

This author is ready to concede that 'much ignorance stems from certain deep-rooted characteristics of "human nature" in politics' but he also argues that there is 'a down-to-earth sense in which an interest in political information *is* natural and could be used as a growth point for the efforts of would-be educators of the democratic citizenry' (p. 99).

The findings of J. D. Halloran (1964), J. G. Blumler and D. McQuail (1968), Colin Seymour-Ure (1974), the Glasgow University Media Group (1976 and 1977) and others make sobering reading and suggest that a number of important changes are necessary if television is to contrbute systematically and constructively to the development of a politically well-informed public. There has been particular criticism of the way in which television reports industrial relations, the allegation being that, perhaps as a result of unconscious bias or a limited appreciation of the complexities of particular issues, a narrow, distorted and one-sided view is presented. Several examples of the kind of reporting being criticised here are presented in the Glasgow studies.

One of these related to the way in which a speech by Harold Wilson, made in 1975 when he was Prime Minister, was extensively used in the television coverage of a strike by 250 engine-tuners at the Cowley plant of British Leyland early in 1975 (Glasgow University Media Group, 1976, ch. 7). On the first day of the strike Mr Wilson made a speech covering a number of areas including government policy on industry and investment. The section of the speech which received most attention from the media was a reference made to 'manifestly avoidable stoppages of production' caused by management and labour. Early BBC bulletins on that day reflected this reference to management *and* unions but later bulletins omitted the reference to management. From the outset, the coverage by ITN presented the Prime Minister's strictures as applying *only* to the workforce. The Glasgow researchers report that: 'On B.B.C. 1 there were 22 references to the strike problem of Leyland as against 5 references to the problem of management and only 1 to investment. On B.B.C. 2 there were 8 references to the strike theme, 3 to management and 2 to investment. On I.T.N. there were 33 to the strike theme, 8 to management and none to investment.' (p. 226.)

The emphasis in this type of reporting is vital because, as Greg Philco and his colleagues observe: 'The way in which stories are presented affects how the events to which they refer are to be seen and understood. Television news, like all journalism, never simply gives "the facts" but always offers a way of understanding the world in which we live.' (Beharrall and Philco, 1977, pp. 1–2.) The Annan Report on Broadcasting made reference to this problem and took the view that 'the broadcasters were not guilty of deliberate and calculated bias. But that the coverage of industrial affairs is in some respects inadequate and unsatisfactory and not in doubt.' The report stated:

They too often forget that to represent the management at their desks, apparently the calm and collected representatives of order, and to represent shop stewards and picket lines stopping production, apparently the agents of disruption, gives a false picture of what strikes are about. The broadcasters have fallen into the professional error of putting compelling camera work before news. (Annan, 1977, p. 272.)

Few bouquets can be awarded for the production of programmes in either radio or television which are specifically designed as ventures in politics for either young people or adults – indeed it has to be said that only a few in this category exist. The first prize must be awarded to Granada Television for their *State of the Nation: Parliament* programmes, presented in 1973 and the *Inside British Politics* series (using much of the earlier material) which was presented in 1977. These added a new dimension to the treatment of politics in television by making dents in the secrecy of the government machine and shedding light in the dark places of the political process, by looking at the political troubles of a wayward MP with his constituency, taking us inside a government department, creating an apparently accurate reconstruction of a Cabinet meeting, and giving glimpses of a local authority and the EEC at work on real problems and issues (see Lapping and Percy, 1973; Mackintosh, 1977b). In the autumn of 1978 Granada screened a television series on political education for 14–16-year-olds under the title of 'Politics: What's It All About?' which was well received in the schools and favourably commented on by many teachers. The programmes have been repeated in subsequent years.

Teacher training

A major barrier to the development of political education lies in the grave shortage of appropriately trained teachers and the virtually complete absence of suitable training courses. Because the need for such teachers is not formally recognised politics is not included in the list of 'shortage subjects', such as Mathematics and Science, as officially defined by the Department of Education and Science. Only a handful of institutions offer any form of training in the teaching of politics at the pre-service level and, thus far, only one institution offers an in-service course leading to a recognised qualification.

A further deficiency, which is important in its overall educational effects, is the fact that, generally, the political perspective is poorly represented in the theoretical studies of education taken by teachers in training (see Brennan, 1978b). This is hardly surprising because the recognition of fundamental political issues and divisions runs counter to the traditions and ethos of training institutions whose task historically was to assist in the process of 'gentling the masses' and to encourage respect for the established social and political order (see e.g. Glass, 1961). Traditional courses in the Theory of Education were, in the main, apolitical, anti-political, or *ersatz* political. There is some evidence that, even when dealing with controversial issues such as the comprehensive-school debate and the role of public schools, many tutors were unaware of the extent to which their own ideological assumptions slanted the nature and form of the discussion. Professor William Taylor has shown how, even when formally encouraging consideration of matters of social concern, the questions raised were confined within strict, non-controversial limits. He makes it clear that the dominant value orientations of teacher educators were 'directed not at the major structural and economic features of society... but the less significant and peripheral working of the larger structures' (Taylor, 1969, pp. 282–3). Danny McDowell has argued that, for a long time, teacher education rested on 'an inherited set of assumptions about the nature and purpose of education' which were largely irrelevant to the contemporary situation. 'In such an ethos,' he suggests, 'there is no place for fundamental disagreement. There is an impatience with politics and political issues, a relentless search for consensus.' (McDowell, 1971, p. 70.)

Nearly forty years ago, the McNair Report on Teacher Training made reference to the desirability of laying 'the foundations of an interest in public affairs and of the practice of being a good citizen' and recognised the value to a college of having on its staff some teachers who have made a special study of the machinery of government, central and local; it also recommended that 'in each training area there should be one or more training institutions which include these matters in their curricula, and an optional subject under the name of social studies, public administration or some similar title' (Board of Education, 1944, p. 68). The only college known to the present writer which seriously attempted to implement this recommendation was the former City of Leeds Training College where, in the early 1950s, there was a compulsory course in Civics. This arrangement presumably derived from the interest and commitment of the then Principal, Dr R. W. Rich, who was the author of a interesting book entitled *The Teacher in a Planned Society* (Rich, 1950).

But more generally for a quarter of a century or more this modest but well-intentioned proposal lay in abeyance. Indeed when Derek Heater surveyed the colleges of education in the late sixties he could find not more than two colleges which offered anything approaching a systematic course in political studies. No college offered a main course in politics and government in its own right; such studies as did exist were to be found in the form of options within other major courses, especially History and Sociology, and owed their existence to the interest and enthusiasm of individual tutors who had to stake their claims against others which were deemed to have more obvious 'legitimacy' and professional relevance (Heater, 1969b; see also Brennan, 1969).

The implementation of the James Report on Teacher Training

(Department of Education and Science, 1972) brought forth a small but vigorous crop of new courses wholly or partly concerned with aspects of government and politics and in a handful of institutions short courses in 'teaching politics' or 'political education' were introduced by the more enthusiastic tutors. However, the spate of retrenchment and reorganisation which followed the draconian reduction of the numbers in teacher training adversely affected these developments and it is, indeed, ironic that one of the effects of reorganisation has been to excise or curtail some of the few developments in this field which were beginning to succeed in establishing themselves.

As the report of the Hansard Society Working Party indicates, the requirements for the development of teacher training include courses which provide for both politics as an academic study (the substance) and as a professional study (the method). It makes a twofold recommendation: professional courses (both pre-service and in-service) must become 'a deliberate matter of policy' and 'Universities and Polytechnics should agree to offer as part of their public responsibility short refresher courses (vacation, evening or half-day release) in the content of their subject to teachers – which is an important and low-cost activity.' (Crick and Porter, 1978, p. 28.) It is recognised that substantial expansion in these fields will necessarily be a gradual development but the way forward is now fairly clear: it remains to be seen if there is the will to provide the means.

The need for further research

The Hansard Society Working Party and the Political Education Research Unit at the University of York were conscious of the limitations in what they had been able to achieve and the short-comings of the research they have been able to undertake. The York Report was more specific about the nature of the tasks which remain and gave important pointers to the direction of future work and research. It recognised, for example, that the political literacy approach itself should be further clarified and refined and related directly to the wider definitions of politics which have been espoused. It suggested that the key working papers (in political literacy, political issues and procedural values) may need to be modified and refined in the light of experience. It is also expressed the belief that more needs to be done to identify and develop the kind of pedagogies appropriate to the political literacy approach; this they regard as 'the major challenge that confronts the political educator in the clasroom'. The report made clear that the project has raised the possibility of the explicit aims in political education in schools being contradicted by the latent assumptions inherent in classroom practice and institutional structures and recommends that teachers and educational planners in Britain should devote far more attention to these questions than they have done hitherto.

They list 'certain key areas' in which further research is needed to improve classroom practice. These include: research into political learning; the use of political concepts by both students and teachers; the use of simulation games; audio-visual approaches to political learning; the analysis and evaluation of discussion techniques; the transmission of values by teachers to students; and the possibilities of using the organisation of the school itself to enhance political learning. If these ends are to be achieved the work necessary would obviously require funding on a generous scale but development based on such knowledge would clearly be more satisfactory than that merely resting on faith and informed speculation (Lister, 1977b, pp. 110–17). If there is to be a basic provision of political education in the common curriculum of all secondary schools as a vital element in educating for a democratic society, there are tasks which must be urgently undertaken and vigorously pursued.

7 Towards a democratic society

'The strength of democracy must be built on refusal to claim to possess the truth, and readiness to arbitrate between conflicting truths by democratic methods, and to the satisfaction of the greatest number. But it must also be willing to be subject to perpetual questioning and challenge.'

Dorothy Pickles (1970)

'The popular belief that people will take up power and responsibility as soon as it is offered to them is not true. People have to be educated in the democratic process.'

Julius Nyerere (quoted in Gauhar, 1979)

Theory and practice

In both politics and education, the historical pattern in England is one of slow, piecemeal and unco-ordinated change. Political and educational systems tend to react to strains, pressures and threats rather than engage in prior planning in efforts to avoid such contingencies. The conservative tradition is deeply entrenched in our institutions and psychology and there is a widespread avoidance of discussion on either abstract ideas or long-term aims. In the education system especially there is, outside of the universities, a deeply ingrained conviction that 'theory' can be separated from 'practice' and that 'practice' is the only really important form of activity. Among practising teachers generally there is a persistent failure to recognise that theory and practice are inseparably linked and reciprocally related. In the wider context, the same is true of the link between ideas and institutions where the reality is, as Bernard Crick aptly puts it, that: 'All ideas seek institutional realisation and institutions embody purposes.' (Crick, 1964, p. 199.) Ideology is not absent because it is not overtly recognised, and, in education, many important values are transmitted by implication rather than by systematic indoctrination.

In relation to the central concerns of this study, which focuses on aspects of the relationship between the educational system and the body politic, no one has recognised this truth more clearly than Karl Mannheim. In their standard *History of Western Education*, William Boyd and Edmund King refer to the 'important contribution' made by Mannheim's 'momentous writings'. They assert: 'His *Diagnosis of Our Time* was a landmark in Western educational thought; and this posthumous *Freedom, Power and Democratic Planning* is pivotal to any proper understanding of the present trends of Western Education in relation to society and politics... It is in relation to industrialized and urbanized conditions that we are most short of guidance; yet it is in this context that Mannheim, and those influenced by him, may be most helpful.' (Boyd and King, 1975, p. 453.)* And yet the work and thought of this important writer have been almost totally ignored in the content of Education courses in the vast majority of teacher-training institutions.

Long before he became professionally concerned with the study of education, Mannheim wrote: 'Sociologists do not regard education solely as a means of realising abstract ideas of culture, such as humanism or technical specialisation, but as part of the process of influencing men and women. Education can only be understood when we know for what kind of society and for what social position the children are being educated.' (Mannheim, 1940, p. 271.) Mannheim was clear about the kind of society which he wanted to achieve. A refugee who came to England after the revolutions in Hungary and the growth of Nazism in Germany, he was passionately concerned to seek a planned change to a more democratic form of society which would avoid the extremes of *laissez-faire* capitalism and totalitarianism. This new pattern of democracy was later to be labelled 'The Third Way' (see Mannheim, 1943).

Mannheim believed that: 'A clear vision of the aims and content of education is all the more desirable as there is a tendency in democracies to discuss problems of organisation rather than ideas, techniques rather than aims. There is no doubt that Democracy has lost a clear conception of the type of citizen it wants to create.' (Mannheim, 1951, p. 199.) He advocated a form of 'social education' and 'the planned use of a wide range of social forces and institutions to create the democratic personality type necessary to guarantee social integration in a reconstructed society' (Floud, 1959, p. 49). The model of 'personality type' he seeks to achieve is set out in *Freedom, Power and Democratic Planning* (p. 199ff) and it is based on

* For general accounts of Mannheim's contribution see W. A. C. Stewart (1953 and 1967) and J. Floud (1959 and 1969).

what H. H. Anderson and H. M. Brewer (1945 and 1946) and D. W. Harding (1940) have called 'integrative behaviour'. Mannheim's conception of integrative behaviour has something in common with the values made explicit in the approach to political education discussed in Chapter 5. He wrote:

> The important element in this conception is that the person...is tolerant of disagreement. He is tolerant not for the sake of compromise, but in the expectation of enlarging his own personality by observing some features of a human being different to himself. Practically this means that the democratic personality welcomes disagreement because it has the courage to expose itself to change.' (Mannheim, 1951, p. 199.)

Mannheim believed that the precondition for the development of democracy, as he conceived it, was consensus. He considered that it would be possible to reach agreement over a wide range of values and that, once agreed, these values could be propagated widely through 'the co-ordination of institutions, education and psychology', and added, 'never, in human history have rulers and decision-makers accumulated such power to do the right thing' (Mannheim, 1943, p. xviii). In this connection, Crick makes the important point that the achievement of consensus is, in itself, a political activity. He writes:

> The *consensus* is not some systematic, external and intangible spiritual adhesive, not some metaphysical cement or something mysteriously prior to or above politics; it is an activity of politics itself...If consensus is simply taken to mean that a high degree of agreement in fact exists about social values...this is more likely to be the *product* of politics than a condition.' (Crick, 1964, p. 177.)

For Mannheim one of the key problems was the lack of social and political awareness. He wrote: 'One of the outstanding problems of the hour is the lack of awareness in social affairs, which in one way is nothing but the lack of a comprehensive sociological orientation.' By 'awareness' he did not mean 'the mere accumulation of rational knowledge. Awareness means both in the life of the individual and in that of the community the readiness to see the whole situation in which one finds onself, and not only to orientate one's action on immediate tasks and purposes but base them on a more comprehensive vision.' The 'political and social realities' must not lie in another dimension beyond the range of his awareness but become part of his sensitivity (Mannheim, 1943, p. 61).

In Mannheim's view education itself had contributed to the suppression of awareness. He castigated the practice of over-specialisation in the schools which had had the effect of 'neutralising the genuine interest in real problems and the possible answers to them'. The universities came in for harsh criticism for their 'mis-interpretation of tolerance and objectivity in terms of neutrality'. For Mannheim neutrality was a mistaken virtue: 'Neither democratic tolerance nor scientific objectivity demand that we should never take a stand for what we believe to be true, nor that we should avoid discussing the final values and objectives of life.' He was concerned that democracies should face up to the vital issues of the day and believed that, in approaching problems of reconstruction, democracy 'has everything to gain and nothing to lose from growing awareness' (Mannheim, 1943, pp. 61–9).

Mannheim saw problems in the process of democratisation in terms of both the perception of the condition of society and the responses to these perceptions. He posited two polarised viewpoints which, he considered, must be reconciled by systematic planning. He advanced the general proposition that thought and attitudes are circumscribed by our position in time and place, and contrasted two distinctive modes of thought which he referred to as 'ideological' and 'utopian' thinking. He stated:

The term 'ideology' reflects the one discovery which emerged from political conflict, namely, that ruling groups can in their thinking become so intensively interest-bound to a situation that they are simply no longer able to see certain facts which would undermine their sense of domination. There is implicit in the word 'ideology' the insight that in certain situations the collective unconscious of certain groups obscures the real condition of society both to itself and to others and thereby stabilizes it.

The concept of 'utopian' thinking reflects the opposite discovery of the political struggle, namely that certain oppressed groups are intellectually so strongly interested in the destruction and transformation of a given situation of society that they unwittingly see only those elements in the situation which tend to negate it. Their thinking is incapable of correctly diagnosing an existing condition of society. They are not at all concerned with what really exists; rather in their thinking they already seek to change the situation that exists. Their thought...can be used only as a direction for action... (Mannheim, 1936, p. 36.)

Each of these perspectives, he argued, is partial and distorts reality; they must be related to form a 'total perspective' which represents objectivity. His analysis is, of course, open to considerable objection both philosophically and sociologically but the point he was making is an important one and at least, it serves to underline the dangers of self-deception from whichever political viewpoint the observation of society is made.

It must be conceded, however, that relevant as Mannheim's thought may be to the theme of educating for democracy, his emphasis on planning, systems and social engineering has done little to commend itself to some educators and critics (see e.g. Bantock, 1952 and 1963; Walsh 1959; Wrong 1961) and the minority of teachers who have become aware of his work. It is clear that sometimes his propensity to abstraction and his concern with 'systems' has led to some misunderstanding and, perhaps, misrepresentation of his regard for the individual personality. W. A. C. Stewart, who prepared much of Mannheim's work for posthumous publication, ascribes to him a central concern that the coherence which he sought should rest upon a 'sense of individuality, the self-awareness of the person and his perception of the relatedness of his ideas and of things' (Mannheim and Stewart, 1962, p. xi).

Mannheim recognised that 'there is need of spiritual power to integrate people' and that 'religion fulfils certain indispensable functions in this age of transition' (Mannheim, 1951, p. 313). W. A. C. Stewart added an important corrective to less sensitive interpretations of Mannheim's thought when he wrote that 'linked with the theme of privacy as a means of individualization he has written of the importance of "paradigmatic experience" in personality structure. By this phrase he means those decisive basic expreiences which are felt to reveal the meaning of life as a whole. Their pattern is so deeply impressed upon our minds that they provide a mould into which other experiences flow, and so they help to shape what we are later to experience.' (Stewart, 1953.)

Cleavage and consensus

Some indication of the possibility of achieving a consensus on the form of democratic society and the pattern of political education appropriate to it can be assessed by examining the attitudes of the major parties to political education. The initial expectation in this might be that Conservatives would stress the role of political education in terms of the need to maintain the political *status quo* and that the Labour Party would be particularly concerned with its contribution to social and political reform.

This, however, is by no means entirely the case. As we have seen (Chapter 4) in the course of the 'Great Debate' a number of the more powerful pressure groups including the CBI and the TUC voiced the need for political education and, during the period of the 1974–9 Labour Government, James Callaghan (as Prime Minister) and Shirley Williams (as Secretary of State for Education and Science) made public expressions of support for the introduction of political education and both Norman St John Stevas and Sir Keith Joseph, then in Opposition, made more qualified but generally approving statements on this theme. Norman St John Stevas (1977) observed:

'There are fundamental values on which our society is based and on which there is general consensus in the democratic parties', and advocated the need 'to build up a consensus among the democratic parties on the approach to the problem of political education'. On both sides there have been discordant voices or expressions of unease but, as we have seen, the Hansard Society proposals were generally well received. In one sense it is, perhaps, surprising that the earliest and most explicit statement on political education by a political party has come from the Conservatives.

In the autumn of 1977, Norman St John Stevas arranged for the establishment of a study group, under the chairmanship of Alan Haslehurst, MP, to consider youth policy. The resulting report appeared in June 1978 in the form of a discussion document entitled *A Time for Youth*. It is clear from this that one of the basic concerns of the group was to find antidotes to 'the frightening prospect of creating a generation, with a significant proportion of minorities, which will be alienated from our society to an extent that we have never before witnessed. This could produce great dangers for the stability of our system and the survival of our democracy.' (Conservative Party Study Group on Youth Policy, 1978, p. 5.) The group produced firm and fairly clear-cut proposals for 'increased provision within the curriculum for forms of political and social education'. The aims of this programme were specified as:

To instil in young people a framework of political values on which they can build.

To help young people develop an awareness of the basic issues which affect the life of the community.

To explain the system by which the nation is governed and how Parliament relates to other institutions, both national and local.

To help young people understanding the international situation and the relations and conflicts between nations.

To give young people a greater knowledge of political facts, such as the composition of government and opposition and the policies advocated by the main political parties.

To teach young people how to make use of the political process so that they can use the system, effect change and make their views heard.
(Conservative Party Study Group on Youth Policy, 1978, pp. 8–9.)

The action proposed to ensure the implementation of this programme was strong and decisive. The group considered that 'the timidity and indecisiveness which presently characterise the attitude of many schools on this point should be roundly condemned'. It expressed the hope that 'local authorities would become increasingly aware of the need to extend this provision' and recommended that: 'Curricular guidelines issued by central government should include these subjects among the "core" to be provided by every secondary school. If local authorities fail to respond, a reserve power should be taken to compel them to do so' (p. 9). These proposals aroused the wrath of such diehards as Woodrow Wyatt, Rhodes Boyson and Nicholas Winterton but they are in stark contrast to those historically pursued and provide a very promising basis for an agreed consensus on the development of political education. The extent to which the action advocated will become officially accepted as Conservative Party policy, of course, remains to be seen.

Although its Parliamentary leaders have given general support to the recommendations on political literacy, the Labour Party, as an organisation, has not as yet made any formal pronouncement on its attitude to political education. Historically, the Labour Party, in pursuit of the ideal of 'Secondary Education for All', has concerned itself with structural changes in the educational system (e.g. the establishment of comprehensive schools) rather than with curriculum content. Individual members have, however, provided occasional exceptions to this general rule and it is worth noting that, in 1939, Hugh Gaitskell, who was later to become leader of the Party, had argued in a publication entitled *Education for Democracy* that 'A more widespread knowledge of the social sciences is especially urgent today. As citizens of a modern democratic community, we are constantly required to pass judgement upon issues to which such knowledge is relevant...Some training in the social sciences is an essential part of education for citizenship.' (Cohen and Travers, 1939.)

In the few instances when the theme of political and social education have been discussed in the post-war era by individuals prominent in the Labour Party or Fabian Society the recipes put forward have been characteristically non-radical. In a contribution to the *New Fabian Essays* which was entitled 'Educational and Social Democracy' Margaret Cole asked: 'What are the essential purposes for a democratic socialist education in the modern world?' She replied that 'by training its recipients in the techiques of social living it must make for self-government, for the capacity to think – and ask the right questions – before acting, for initiative and the growth of leadership, and for the sense of responsibility and sense of public service, which, however difficult they may be to define or consciously to "inculcate" are the essentials of democratic society' (M. Cole, 1952, p. 105). Margaret Cole, however, seemed to accept that 'questions of technique and curriculum have to be left largely in the hands of those who will have to do the work' (p. 107) and that problems of organisation of the educational structure loomed larger than those of curriculum content.

Anthony Crosland's book, *The Future of Socialism* (1956), 'had little to say about education at the theoretical level' and 'although the book as a whole was important,...the sections on education are by far the weakest and most conservative' (Lawton, 1978, p. 140). This author concludes that: 'There have been no socialist theorists of education within the Labour Party' and expresses the view that the formulating of such a theory is vitally necessary to the development of democratic society. As Lawton points out: 'Whether you want to change society in a particular way or leave it as it is...is a political stance; whether you want to educate *all* people or only some of them is a reflection of social and political values' (p. 171).

More recently greater interest in political education has been shown by individuals and groups within the Labour Party. In 1978, the Young Fabians sought an author for a pamphlet on political education and the Young Socialists called on the National Executive Committee to include a commitment to political education in the Party Programme. Neil Kinnock, MP, who is currently Opposition spokesman on Education, devoted part of his Parliamentary secretarial and research allowance to a study of political education and he concluded that 'political education in schools is one of the few ways in which ordinary people can learn about their rights and how to organise collectively'. He saw education for citizenship as the 'provision for englightenment and for change' (Whitty, 1978, p. 7).

Reservations and radical critiques

Whitty reports that some individual members of the Labour Party and radical thinkers have expressed strong reservations about the Hansard Society recommendations on political literacy and are either cautious or forthrightly sceptical about its intentions and likely effects. Caroline Benn feels that there are dangers in latching on to the school timetabling of political education 'when its nature and implications have hardly been thought through'. She believes that in practice, formal political education involving a centrally agreed syllabus would be 'so bland and circumscribed as to be useless' and it could all too easily become a form of conservative indoctrination which serves to reinforce these tendencies which are already inherent in the 'hidden' curriculum (Whitty, 1978, p. 7).

Reference has already been made to the critique of the Hansard Society proposals by writers such as Tapper and Salter (see Chapter 1) who share with Pamela Jones the view that the political literacy programme could be conceived of as 'a way of establishing hegemony...in this new phase of corporate capitalism' (Whitty, 1978, p. 5). Tapper and Salter state: 'Our objections centre on their failure to challenge the traditional relationship between social class and the British education system...There is nothing in the proposals for political education to suggest that this is likely to be disturbed. In fact, like social education, it is in danger of being labelled as an attempt to place that class control on a firmer and more subtle basis.' (Tapper and Salter, 1978, p. 84.) The prospect for political education seen by these writers is a dismal one. They suggest that the advocates of the political literacy 'have missed the boat...They have come into the arena at the end of a great wave of educational, including curriculum innovations and, unfortunately from their point of view, they are likely to be swamped by the growing reaction to the alleged excesses and failings of these innovations' (p. 87).

Tapper and Salter make an important comparison between the Hansard Society proposals and the explicit programme of political education in the USA and the USSR. They also raise the vital question as to whether the school, as such, is capable of influencing changes in society. They observe:

In both the United States and the U.S.S.R. the state relies upon several other agents of political indoctrination besides formal education. Furthermore the schools share their politically educative function with at least an élite consensus on what forms of citizenship should be perpetuated. In a sense the school is a redundant agent of political education for it has a consensus imposed upon it (rather than creating the consensus itself) and it reinforces the messages transmitted by other powerful socialising forces. It is most decidedly not an innovator. If there is a crisis of citizenship in the United Kingdom...then the experiences of the United States or the Soviet Union would not encourage one to seek a solution in formal political education. The battles have to be decided elsewhere and then, for what it is worth, formal political education will emerge. (Tapper and Salter, 1978, p. 87.)

Socialists and radicals who accept the validity of this type of analysis, and there is a mass of literature to support it (see e.g. Bowles and Gintis, 1976; Davies, 1976; W. Tyler, 1977), are faced with a dilemma. Shorn of sophisticated intellectual argument, the question is whether, short of major changes in political attitudes and institutional structures in society, there is any point in attempting to bring about gradual change via the medium of educational innovation? For these people the answer must, perhaps, lie in a judgement on the worthwhileness, or otherwise, of an attempt to share in slow, gradual and limited changes that at least tend in the direction in which it is hoped that society will move. Some relevant comments were made by the radical educator Paulo Freire, when in conversation with Ian Lister at the University of York.* The general tenor of Freire's

* The text of this discussion is available from Documentation Service, Department of Education, University of York, Heslington, York,, YO1 5DD.

observations is one of hope rather than despair. He says in answer to Lister's question:

It depends on, once again, the political approach which the schools have, whom the schools are serving, against whom the schools are working. This is for me the question. Anyway, we are working inside institutions. Sometimes we are tactically inside the institutions and strategically outside the institutions. And it explains also our ambiguity sometimes. We cannot escape from this ambiguity.

The question is, then, to discover some open space inside the institutions – this sub-system of education which we have – in order to use them. But, once again, the very research of this open space demands from us a certain political clarity, because when I am looking for some open space inside the institutions I have to know *why* I am looking for this open space, and *for what*. It's not a methodological question, but it is a political question. For what do I need some open space in order to work? What am I to do, and with whom in this space? I am not pessimistic, and I think we can do some good things inside universities.

Geoff Whitty has faced this question. He observes that 'the political literacy approach does, at least, provide the right to present socialist ideas alongside conservative ones and it is much easier to demand a "right of reply" when a bias is explicit than when it is merely an implicit feature of institutional life'. He also believes that 'there are aspects of the movement towards a closer relationship between school and the world outside which can be genuinely progressive, or, more accurately, that there are features of an essentially reactionary initiative which can be turned to radical ends' (Whitty, 1978, p. 8).

The historical record shows that attitudes to political education have changed since the turn of the century, even if this is presently more evident in rhetoric than in practical reality. It would be a pity if the genuinely-held beliefs of more radical observers were to lessen the effort and enthusiasm of those teachers who were willing to see what could be achieved. This statement, however, in no way suggests that the schools alone can create the conditions for the betterment of society and progress towards a genuinely democratic system. If, however, there were a genuine and widespread desire to effect change in these directions, education, along with other agencies, would have an important role to play.

Democracy and participation

Expressions of support for the introduction of political education from front-rank politicians of both major parties have, regrettably, been advanced largely for negative reasons. If political education for democratic society is to be genuinely pursued, the response by government must be unmistakably positive and give evidence of a realistic and determined desire for change. This would involve a readiness to look at the condition of contemporary society and the manifest inequalities that exist with a view to removing the starker disparities in wealth and status and establishing the democratic machinery through which this could be done. G. D. H. Cole (1920) pointed to the shortcomings of 'the abstract democracy of the ballot box', and argued that 'vast inequalities' are 'necessarily fatal to any real democracy, whether in politics or any other sphere'.

It has already been argued that there is a growing disillusion with democracy as currently practised and that this expresses itself in a variety of forms, not least in an apathy and cynicism based on the assumption that government, and its vast array of bureaucratic structures, has become increasingly remote from the governed. Carole Pateman (1970) suggests that 'the contemporary theory of democracy represents a considerable failure of the political and sociological imagination' because it leaves out of account the important ingredients of personal involvement and public participation. She shows that the received view of democracy concentrates on the representative elements and ascribes only minimal participation to the people, some theorists indeed seeing widespread political involvement as positively dangerous. In her critique of classical democratic theory Pateman examines the work of B. R. Berelson *et al.* (1954), R. A. Dahl (1956), H. Eckstein (1966) and G. Sartori (1962), all of whom place a heavy emphasis on the need for stability in the political system. She writes:

Berelson's work provides us with a clear statement of some of the main arguments of recent work in democratic theory...From this standpoint we can see that high levels of participation and interest are required from a minority of citizens only and, moreover, the apathy and disinterest of the majority play a valuable role in maintaining the stability of the system as a whole. Thus we arrive at the argument that the amount of participation that actually obtains is just about the amount that is required for a stable system of democracy. (Pateman, 1970, p. 7.)

The argument that the fundamental stability of a democratic system must depend on widespread political inactivity (see e.g. Morris-Jones, 1964) is, surely, both politically defeatist and morally untenable. The classical theory of democracy has undoubtedly been politically and intellectually dominant but it is only one alternative in democratic thought and practice. An alternative perspective, represented most notably by John Stuart Mill, Rousseau and G. D. H. Cole, places a much greater emphasis on the necessity of individual and group participation as the distinguishing feature of a democratic polity.

The advocates of increased participation in the affairs of a democratic society stress the educational and integrative effects of political involvement. G. M. Higgins and J. J. Richardson observe: 'When Aristotle described man as a political animal, he meant that man realised himself fully only when participating in self government. The goal of participationists thus becomes not merely participation in government, but a participatory *society*. Democracy is no longer seen as a means of good government but as an end in itself.' (Higgins and Richardson, 1976, p. 6.) The participatory society is concerned not only with the effectiveness of the machinery of government but the development of the human personality.

Carole Pateman (1970, ch. 2) traces the contributions to this theme in the writings of Rousseau, J. S. Mill and G. D. H. Cole, J. S. Mill, she reminds us, considered that government is 'a great influence acting on the human mind', and that his criteria for the judgement of governmental institution is 'the degree to which they promote the general mental advancement of the community, including under that phrase, advancement in intellect, in virtue and in practical activity and efficiency' (Mill, 1910, p. 195). Rousseau's prescription for the ideal relationship between the citizen and government is educative in the widest sense. It is designed, says Pateman, 'to develop responsible, individual social and political actions through the effect of the participatory process...As a result of participating in decision-making the individual is educated to distinguish between his own impulses and desires; he learns to be a public as well as a private citizen.' (Pateman, 1970, pp. 24 and 25.)

G. D. H. Cole argued that 'democracy is only real when it is conceived in terms of function and purpose', and pointed to the educative and integrative deficiencies of the representative system: 'having chosen his representative, the ordinary man has, according to that theory, nothing left to do except let other people govern him'. In contrast, a system of 'functional' representation implies 'the constant participation of the ordinary man in the conduct of those parts of the structure of society with which he is directly concerned, and which he has therefore the best chance of understanding' (G. D. H. Cole, 1920a, p. 114). All of this remains part of what Davis (1964) has called 'the unfinished business of democracy' which requires 'the elaboration of plans of action and specific prescriptions which offer hope of progress towards a genuinely democratic polity' (quoted in Pateman, 1970, p. 21). Carole Pateman's survey concludes with the observation that: 'neither the demands for participation, nor the theory of participatory democracy itself, are based...on dangerous illusions or an outmoded theoretical foundation'. She believes that: 'We can still have a modern, viable system of democracy which retains the notion of participation at its heart.' (p. 111).

An American writer, Sherry R. Arnstein, expresses very positively what he deems to be the purposes of participation in the decision-making process:

Citizen participation is a categorical term for citizen power that enables the have-not citizens, presently excluded from the political and economic processes, to be deliberately included in the future. It is the strategy by which the have-nots join in determining how information is shared, goals and policies are set, tax resources are allocated, programmes are operated, and benefits...are parcelled out. In short, it is the means by which they can induce significant social reform which enables them to share in the benefits of the affluent society.

This writer also makes careful distinction between degrees of participation which represent more 'tokenism' and those which involve 'effective power and influence' (Arnstein, 1969).

Discussion of the virtues of political participation became fashionable in Britain in the 1960s. The idea, basically, was that a healthy, developing democracy demands a more widespread involvement of citizens 'taking part in the formulation, passage or implementation of public policies' (Parry, 1972, p. 5), instead of being merely passive recipients of decisions made by others on matters which affect their daily lives. The notion received particular attention in the field of planning. In 1965 a Planning Advisory Group was set up by the Ministry of Housing and Local Government and this reported that there had been inadequate participation by the individual citizen in the planning process and insufficient regard to his interest. This led to the establishment of a committee to investigate possible methods of obtaining such participation with a view to making provision for more democratic planning procedures. The result was the Skeffington Report on *People and Planning* published in 1969. It is worth noting that this report took acount of the educational implications of participation. It stated:

The same authority will often be both local planning authority and local education authority...We recommend that where the authorities are the same, the closest possible liaison should be kept between these two departments in order that knowledge about the physical planning of the community may be available as part of the outward-looking curriculum which has been recommended in several reports on education...Lessons on such subjects will come to life more vividly when children feel involved. Senior classes should be encouraged to attend exhibitions illustrating either structure plans or local plans for the area in which their school is situated. The education of secondary children about aspects of community life offers the best foundation for worthwhile participation in the years to come. (See Skeffington, 1969, para. 244–7.)

But, generally, public involvement in participation has been extremely limited. Elected office-holders and administrators alike have been concerned to safeguard what they see as their proper prerogatives and disinclined to submit themselves to the kind of searching inquiry which such participation frequently involves. Participation procedures are undoubtedly time-consuming and pre-suppose that the 'expert' view is open to alteration in the light of convincing argument. It is also true that where such procedures have been seriously embarked upon it can be shown that the experts are not omniscient and that ordinary people can make an important contribution to enlightened decision-making and the creation of a more satisfied community. J. R. Lucas suggests that participation is a 'politic policy' which will generally result in making a community 'have more of a common mind about more things'. He adds: 'It is also a policy which manifests a deep respect for the opinion of each of its members, and exemplifies the two ideals of justice and freedom, which are fundamental to any understanding of the state.' (Lucas, 1976, p. 248.)

Among the political parties in recent years, the Liberals have been most consistent in advocating a wider degree of political and industrial participation and Liberals at the local level have demon-strated some of the problems and possibilities of 'community politics'. The Labour Party, to which advocates of participation are most likely to look for a lead, has, somewhat belatedly and as yet only formally, recognised the dangers of the growth of insensitive bureaucracies and the lack of involvement. In a foreword to the Labour Party manifesto for the 1979 General Election the then leader, Jim Callaghan, stated as a 'basic consideration': 'Our policy will tilt the balance of power back to the individual and the neighbourhood, and away from the bureaucrats of town hall, company board room, the health service and Whitehall.' (Labour Party, 1979, p. 4.) It must be confessed, however, that except for the proposals on industrial participation the text took little cognisance of this premise in the plans actually put forward.

It is encouraging that, in the aftermath of Labour's defeat in 1979, some individual MPs have taken this message to heart. No fewer than three Fabian Society* tracts which followed each other in quick succession within a few months of the electoral defeat addressed themselves, in part at least, to the theme of participation. In one of these Austin Mitchell states:

* The Fabian Society 'exists to further socialist education and research. It is affiliated to the Labour Party, both nationally and locally, and embraces all shades of socialist opinion, within its ranks...'

We have to update our traditional approaches to build a better, freer and more equal society. This means recognising the reaction which has taken place against monoliths and the deadening, money-absorbing bureaucracies they have spawned. We must recognise the problems of scale and need for intimacy and involvement. We need to mobilise the dynamic forces in society whether they be economic, social or simple self-help. Government has to work with them, tap their energies for broader social purposes and help them to produce a genuine partnership which mobilises energy and commitment. (Mitchell, 1979, p. 20.)

Other statements making clear a rejection of the unintended consequences of large-scale organisation and the need for involvement have been made by Giles Radice (1980, pp. 4–5) and Evan Luard (1980, p. 24).

The Conservative Party manifesto of 1979 had little to say on participation beyond a passing reference to a 'possible Bill of Rights'. In the context of industrial participation, the main preoccupation seemed to lie in a desire to curb the power of the trade unions. The document stated: 'We welcome closer involvement of workers whether trade unionists or not, in the decisions that affect them in their place of work. It would be wrong to impose by law a system of participation in every company. It would be equally wrong to use the pretext of encouraging worker involvement in order simply to increase union power or facilitate union control of pension funds.' (Conservative Party, 1979, p. 11.)

The failure of recent governments is not only a failure to solve economic problems, it is a failure to recognise and act upon the sociological and psychological facts that human beings do not necessarily or voluntarily accord to the model of 'economic man'. There is more to human dignity than material well-being, important though this is. Democracy implies that institutions should adapt to human needs rather than that men and women should be required to adjust to the frequently insensitive procedures and practices of governmental organisations. Against such practices there are, outside of the inadequate consumer councils of the nationalised industries and the cumbersome procedures in making representations to the Parliamentary, Local and Health Service Commissioners, no readily available forms of redress against the pettiness and incompetence to which citizens are sometimes subjected. If, as Jim Callaghan says in the Labour Party manifesto, 'Industrial democracy – giving working men and women a voice in the decisions which affect their jobs – is an idea whose time has come' (Labour Party, 1979, p. 4), this is no less true for participation in other spheres of life. Participation requires appropriate knowledge, skills and attitudes and a useful beginning might be made in a determined attempt to develop these requirements through political education in the schools.

Future prospect

The political theory of participatory democracy is also an educational theory in the widest sense of the term. This educational theory is one which has a high degree of congruence with the kind of knowledge, attitudes and skills which form the basis of the political literacy approach to political education. A widespread agreement on the desirability of moving in this direction would greatly enhance the possibility of achieving a pattern of democratic organisation which would have greater legitimacy and would command a much greater degree of public support. What then are the possibilities of bringing about this fundamental change?

Conservative politicans have become increasingly concerned about the continuing stability of the political system which has for so long catered effectively for the interests of elite groups; they must recognise that the in-built inegalitarianism of the existing structure cannot indefinitely be sustained. Labour politicians have preached the need for the creation of a more egalitarian society but, in successive periods in office, have succeeded only marginally in denting the traditional differentiation in the allocation of wealth, power and status. The probability is that they have taken too much for granted the traditional mode of government and relied too much on a machinery of government which reflects the interests of a *status quo* outlook on society.

Under Mrs Thatcher's leadership, the Conservative Party has abandoned its traditional Toryism and moved firmly to the right; in the Labour Party, the influence of the left appears to be stronger than at any time in the post-war period. The result is that political divisions are wide and bitter. The alternatives propounded are clear but neither seems likely to command widespread electoral support. Neither group has been prepared to ask fundamental questions about the nature of democracy and continuing signs of disquiet and disillusion on the part of ordinary people, for whom the partisan struggle seems remote, are apparent.

The founders of the Council for Social Democracy were at least aware of this problem. The so-called 'Limehouse Declaration', published on 25 January 1981, states: 'There must be more decentralisation of decision making in industry and government, together with an effective and practical system of democracy at work. The quality of our public and community services must be improved and they must be made more responsive to people's needs.' Whether or not the proposed new party will gain sufficient electoral support for this statement of belief to be put to the practical test remains to be seen.

One way in which society has changed in the last few decades is that there is a much higher level of expectation about the responsibilities of government (see King, 1976). The fact that these responsibilities in the main tend to be seen as material rather than moral reflects the divisiveness which the existing form of society perpetuates rather than any inherent deficiency in human nature. In the absence of any fundamental change in the social and political structure, or at least manifest and determined moves in this direction, it is difficult to see any alternative to the pattern of periodic confrontation on economic issues and a deepening cynicism about the body politic. If moral vision fails, practical demands of a more critical kind may hasten the process of societal review. Part of the answer is likely to be found in a pattern of democracy more in keeping with modern trends and needs, which is much more egalitarian in nature and pays more than lip-service to the ideal of social justice.

This brings us back to the complex question of the basic consensus. Karl Mannheim saw democracy as 'essentially a method of social change, the institutionalisation of the belief that adjustment to changing reality and the reconciliation of diverse interests could be brought about by conciliatory means, with the help of discussion, bargaining and integral consensus.' (Mannheim, 1943, p. 69.) Perhaps in our present troubled situation, we should summon the courage to put this to the test?

We would, clearly, need to go beyond the customary rhetoric and cosmetic cliches: fundamental discussion on the issue of political education would provide an interesting starting point. It has been repeatedly stressed that political education cannot be a panacea and it should not be used as an attempt to paper over the basic divisions of viewpoint in our society. Nevertheless, the existence of clearly defined policies approved by the major parties would indicate the extent of agreement and discord in this important area and provide the means by which their concern and determination to pursue democratic ideals and practices could be soberly examined and assessed.

Bibliography

This bibliography contains all the works which are cited in the text together with further sources to which reference was made in preparing it.

Abrams, M. (1967), 'Social Trends and Electoral Behaviour', in R. Rose (ed.), *Studies in British Politics*, Macmillan.

Abramson, P. (1967), 'The Differential Political Socialisation of English School Children', *Sociology of Education*, vol. 40, no. 3.

Almond, G. and Verba, S. (1963). *The Civic Culture*, Princeton University Press.

Anderson, H. H. and Brewer, H. M. (1945 and 1946), 'Studies in Teachers' Classroom Personalities', *Applied Psychology Monographs of the American Psychological Society*, nos, 6, 8 and 11, Stanford University Press.

Allen, G. (1979), 'Researching Political Education Programmes in Schools and Colleges: a Description of some of the activities of the Political Education Research Unit at the University of York, England, 1974–77', *International Journal of Political Education*, vol. 2, no. 1, and vol. 2, no. 2.

Annan, Lord (chmn) (1977), Chairman, *Report of the Committee on the Future of Broadcasting*, Cmd 6753, HMSO.

Arnstein, S. R. (1969), 'A Ladder of Citizen Participation', *Journal of American Institute of Planners*, July 1969.

Ashton, J. (1977), *Grassroots*, Quartet Books.

Association for Education in Citizenship (1935), *Education for Citizenship in Secondary Schools*, Oxford University Press.

Azrael, J. (1965), 'Soviet Union', in J. Coleman (ed.), *Educational and Political Development*, Princeton University Press.

Bachrach, P. and Baratz, N. (1970), *Power and Poverty*, Oxford University Press.

Bagehot, W. (1963), *The English Constitution*, Fontana.

Balfour, Earl of (1927), Introduction to W. Bagehot, *The English Constitution*.

Banks, O. (1968), *The Sociology of Education*, Batsford.

Bantock, G.H. (1952), *Freedom and Authority in Education*, Faber.

—— (1963), *Education in an Industrial Society*, Faber.

—— (1968), *Culture, Industrialisation and Education*, Routledge and Kegan Paul.

Barnes, D., Britton, J. and Rosen, H. (1969), *Language, Learner and The School*, Penguin.

Beer, S. (1965), *Modern British Politics*, Faber and Faber.
Beharrell, P. and Philco, H. (eds.) (1977), *Trade Unions and the Media*, Macmillan.
Benedict, R. (1968), *Patterns of Culture*, Routledge and Kegan Paul.
Benn, S. I. and Peters, R. S. (1959), *Social Principles and The Democratic State*, Allen and Unwin.
Berelson, B. R., Lazarfeld, P. F. and McPhee, W. N. (1954), *Voting*, University of Chicago Press.
Blondel, J. (1975), *Voters, Parties and Leaders* (revd edn), Penguin.
Blumler, J. G. (1974), 'Does Political Ignorance Matter?', *Teaching Politics*, vol. 3, no. 3.
Blumler, J. G. and McQuail, D. (1968), *Television in Politics: Its Uses and Influence*, Faber and Faber.
Board of Education (1910), *The Code and Suggestions for the Consideration of Teachers and Others Concerned in the Work of Public Elementary Schools 1909–1910 (School Government Handbook no. VI)*, The School Government Chronicle and Educational Authorities Gazette.
—— (1926), *Report of the Consultative Committee on the Education of the Adolescent*, HMSO.
—— (1938a), *Report of the Consultative Committee on Primary Education*, HMSO.
—— (1938b), *Report of the Consultative Committee on Secondary Education with Special Reference to Grammar Schools and Technical High Schools*, HMSO.
—— (1943), *Curriculum and Examinations in Secondary Schools: Report of the Committee of the Secondary Schools Examination Council*, HMSO.
—— (1944), *Teachers and Youth Leaders: Report of the Committee Appointed by the President of the Board of Education to Consider the Supply, Recruitment and Training of Teachers and Youth Leaders*, HMSO.
Boyd, W. and King, E. J. (1975), *The History of Western Education* (11th edn), Adam and Charles Black.
Bowles, S. and Gintis, H. (1976), *Schooling in Capitalist America*, Routledge and Kegan Paul.
Boyson, R. (1978), 'There is More to Life than Learning about Politics', *The Times*, 31 January 1978.
Brennan, T. (1961), 'Teaching for International Understanding in a Secondary Modern School', *Researches and Studies*, no. 21, Institute of Education, University of Leeds.
—— (1963), 'Teaching for International Understanding and the Curriculum of Secondary Schools' in H. Serden (ed.), *Education for International Understanding under Conditions of Tension*, UNESCO, Institute for Education, Hamburg.
—— (1969), 'Studying Politics in a College of Education', *Education and Social Science*, vol. 1, no. 2.
—— (1972a), *Politics and Government in Britain: an Introductory Survey*, Cambridge University Press.
—— (1972b), 'Political Studies in Secondary Schools', *Teaching Politics*, vol. 1, no. 1.
—— (1974), *Political Studies: a Handbook for Teachers*, Longman.

—— (1977a), 'Political Education and the Curriculum: Official Attitudes and Pronouncements, 1900–1977' in I. Lister (ed.), *Report of Political Education Research Unit*, University of York.

—— (1977b), 'British Government and Politics for the Secondary School', *Parliamentary Affairs*, vol. 32, no. 3.

—— (1978a), 'Television and Politics', *Political Quarterly*, vol. 49, no. 3.

—— (1978b), 'Political Education and Teacher Training', in B. Crick and A. Porter (eds.), *Political Education and Political Literacy*, Longman.

—— (1980), 'Political Education and "A Framework for the School Curriculum"', *Teaching Politics*, vol. 9, no. 3.

—— (1981), 'Politics and the Curriculum', in B. Dufour (ed.), *New Movements in the Social Sciences and Humanities*, Temple Smith.

Brennan, T. and Brown, J. (eds.) (1975), *Political Education: Problems and Perspectives*, BBC Publications.

Brennan, T. and Willcock, J. B. (1962), 'The Modern World: a Composite Course of Modern Studies for Secondary Schools', in B. Ford and J. L. Henderson (eds.), *The Living Past*, Institute of Education, University of Sheffield.

Brennan, T., Cooney, S. W. and Pollins, H. (1954), *Social Change in South West Wales*, Watts.

Broudy, H. S. (1962), 'To Regain Educational Leadership', *Studies in Philosophy of Education*, no. 11.

Brown, J. F. (1975), 'Bias', in T. Brennan and J. F. Brown (eds.), *Teaching Politics: Problems and Perspectives*, BBC Publications.

Bryant, M. E. (1965), 'Education for Citizenship in England', *Paedagogische Studien*, Mannblad Voor Orderwijs en Oproeding, Jaargang 42.

Burston, W. H. (1948), 'History and Education in Citizenzhip', *History*, October 1948.

—— (1962), *Social Studies and the History Teacher*, Historical Association.

Butler, D. and Kavanagh, D. (1980), *The British General Election of 1979*, Macmillan.

Clarke, F. (1946), *Freedom in the Educative Society*, University of London Press.

Cohen, J. I. and Travers, R. M. W. (eds.) (1939), *Education for Democracy*, Macmillan.

Cole, G. D. H. (1920a), *Social Theory*, Methuen.

—— (1920b), *Guild Socialism Restated*, Leonard Parsons.

Cole, M. (1952), 'Education and Social Democracy', in R. Crossman (ed.), *New Fabian Essays*, Turnstile Press.

Connell, R. W. (1971), *The Child's Construction of Politics*, Melbourn University Press.

Conservative Party, *The Conservative Manifesto, 1979*, Conservative Central Office.

Conservative Party Study Group on Youth Policy (1978), *A Time for Youth*, Conservative Central Office.

Cosin, B. R. (ed.) (1972), *Education: Structure and Society*, Penguin.

Coxall, W. N. (1973), *Politics: Compromise and Conflict in a Liberal Democracy*, Pergamon.

Crewe, I., Alt, J. and Sarlvik, B. (1977), 'Partisan De-alignment in Britain, 1964–74', *British Journal of Political Science*, vol. 7, no. 2.

Crick, B. (1964), *In Defence of Politics*, Penguin.

—— (1966), 'The Tendency of Political Studies', *New Society*, 3 November 1966.

—— (1969), 'The Introducing of Politics', in D. B. Heater (ed.), *The Teaching of Politics*, Methuen.

—— (1971), *Political Theory and Practice*, Allen Lane, The Penguin Press.

—— (1975), 'Chalk-dust, Punch-card and the Polity', *Political Studies*, vol. 23, no. 283.

—— (1977), 'Education and the Polity', Inaugural Lecture, Birkbeck College, University of London, 20 January 1977.

Crick, B. and Heater, D. B. (1977), *Essays on Political Education*, Falmer Press.

Crick, B. and Porter, A. (eds.) (1978), *Political Education and Political Literacy*, Longman.

Crosland, A. (1956), *The Future of Socialism*, Cape.

Crossman, R. H. S. (ed.) (1952), *New Fabian Essays*, Turnstile Press.

Dahl, R. R. (1956), *Preface to Democratic Theory*, University of Chicago Press.

Davies, B. (1976), *Social Control and Education*, Methuen.

Davis, L. (1964), 'The Cost of Realism: Contemporary Restatements of Democracy', *Western Political Quarterly*, vol. 18.

Dawson, R. E. and Prewitt, K. (1969), *Political Socialisation*, Little Brown.

Department of Education and Science (1967), *Towards World History*, Pamphlet no. 52, HMSO.

—— (1972), *Teacher Education and Training: a Report by a Committee of Inquiry Appointed by the Secretary of State for Education and Science, under the Chairmanship of Lord James of Rusholme*, HMSO.

—— (1977), *Education in Schools*, HMSO.

—— (1979a), *The Curriculum 11–16: Working Papers by H.M. Inspectors*, HMSO.

—— (1979b), *Local Authority Arrangements for the School Curriculum*, HMSO.

—— (1980a), *A View of the Curriculum*, HMSO.

—— (1980b), *A Framework for the School Curriculum*, HMSO.

Dewey, J. (1915), *The School and Society* (2nd edn), Cambridge University Press.

—— (1916), *Democracy and Education*, Macmillan.

Dickson, A. (1975), Foreword to S. Goodlad (ed.), *Education and Social Action*, Allen and Unwin.

Dowse, R. S. and Hughes, J. A. (1971), 'The Family, The School, and the Political Socialisation Process', *Sociology*, vol. 5, no. 1.

—— (1975), *Political Sociology*, John Wiley.

Dray, J. and Jordan, D. (1950), *A Handbook of Social Studies for Teachers in Secondary Schools and County Colleges*, Methuen.

Durbin, E. F. M. (1940), *The Politics of a Democratic Socialism*, Routledge and Kegan Paul.

Easton, D. and Dennis, J. (1969), *Children in the Political System*, McGraw-Hill.

Eckstein, H. (1966), 'A Theory of Stable Democracy', Appendix B of *Division and Cohesion in Democracy*, Princeton University Press.

Economics Association (1977), *The Contribution of Economics to General Education: Report by an Ad Hoc Committee.*

Elcock, H. (1976), *Political Behaviour*, Methuen.

Elkin, F. (1960), *The Child and Society*, Random House.

Entwistle, H. (1971), *Political Education in a Democracy*, Routledge and Kegan Paul.

——(1974), 'Education and the Concept of Political Socialisation', *Teaching Politics*, vol. 3, no. 2.

Farnen, R. F. and German, D. B. (1972), 'Youth, Politics and Education', in B. B. Massialas (ed.), *Political Youth, Traditional Schools*, Prentice Hall.

Floud, J. (1959), 'Karl Mannheim', in A. V. Judges, *The Function of Teaching*, Faber and Faber.

—— (1969), 'Karl Mannheim', in T. Raison (ed.), *The Founding Fathers of Social Science*, Penguin.

Frankenberg, R. (1966), *Communities in Britain*, Penguin.

Freedman, L. (1974), 'Approaching Politics', *Teaching Politics*, vol. 3, no. 1.

Gardner, W. (1969), 'Political Socialisation', in D. B. Heater (ed.), *The Teaching of Politics*, Methuen.

Gauhar, A. (1979), 'The Teacher Plans for End of Term', *Guardian*, 8 January 1979.

Gilmour, I. (1969), *The Body Politic*, Hutchinson.

Giner, S. (1972), *Sociology*, Martin Robertson.

Glasgow University Media Group (1976), *Bad News*, Routledge and Kegan Paul.

—— (1977), *More Bad News*, Routledge and Kegan Paul.

Glass, D. V. (1961), 'Education and Social Change in Modern England', in A. H. Halsey and J. Floud (eds.), *Education, Economy and Society*, Collier-Macmillan.

Golby, M. and Rush, M. (1980), *Education for Democracy (Political Education): an Interim Report*, Devon Local Education Authority.

Grant, N. (1969), 'Teacher Training in the U.S.S.R. and Western Europe', *Report of Conference of Comparative Education Society of Europe, British Section*, University of Reading.

Greenslade, R. (1979), *Goodbye to the Working Class*, Marion Boyars.

Greenstein, F. (1965), *Children and Politics*, Yale University Press.

Groombridge, B. (1972), *Television and the People*, Penguin.

Gross, N., Glacquinta, J. B. and Berstein, M. (1971), *Implementing Organizational Innovations: a Sociological Analysis of Planned Educational Change*, Harper and Row.

Guttsman, W. (1968), *The British Political Elite*, MacGibbon and Kee.

Halloran, J. D. (1964), *The Effects of Mass Communication with Special Reference to Television*, Leicester University Press.

Halsey, A. H. and Floud, J. (eds.) (1961), *Education, Economy and Society*, Collier-Macmillan.

Harding, D. W. (1940), 'The Custom of War and the Notion of Peace', *Scrutiny*, vol. 9, no. 3.

Heater, D. B. (1969a), 'Political Studies in Schools – Some Problems', *Education and Social Science*, vol. 1, no. 2.
—— (1969b), *The Teaching of Politics*, Methuen.
—— (1972a), 'History Teaching and Political Education', *History*, vol. 57.
—— (1972b), 'Political Education in Schools', *Teaching Politics*, vol. 1, no. 1.
—— (1976), 'International Studies at School Level', *British Journal of International Studies*, no. 2.
—— (1978), 'A Burgeoning of Interest: Political Education in Britain', *International Journal of Political Education*, vol. 1, no. 4.
—— (1979), *Essays on Contemporary Studies*, G. W. & A. Hesketh.
—— (1980), *World Studies: Education for International Understanding in Britain*, Harrap.
Hemming, J. (1949), *The Teaching of Social Studies in Secondary Schools*, Longman.
Hennessy, R. and Slater, J. (1977), 'Political Competence', *The Times Educational Supplement*, 25 November 1977 and (1978) in B. Crick and A. Porter (eds.), *Political Education and Political Literacy*, Longman.
Henriques, L. F. (1954), 'Subcultures in English Society', *Researches and Studies*, no. 6, Institute of Education, University of Leeds.
Hess, R. D. (1968), 'Political Socialisation in the Schools', *Harvard Educational Review*, vol. 38, no. 3.
Hess, R. D. and Torney, J. V. (1967), *The Development of Political Attitudes in Children*, Aldine Press.
Higgins, G. M. and Richardson, J. J. (1976), *Political Participation*, Politics Association.
Hill, D. M. (1970), *Participating in Local Affairs*, Penguin.
Hipkin, J. (1976), 'The Curriculum (11–16): What it is and what it might be', Department of Education, University of York.
Hirst, P. S. & Peters, R. S. (1970), *The Logic of Education*, Routledge and Kegan Paul.
Houghton, Lord (chmn) (1976), *Report of the Committee on Financial Aid to Political Parties*, Cmd 6601, HMSO.
Hughes, A. G. (1951), *Education and the Democratic Ideal*, Longman.
Hyman, H. (1959), *Political Socialisation*, Free Press.
Inkeles, A. (1964), *What is Sociology?*, Prentice Hall.
Jackson, R. (1973), 'Political Education in the European Economic Community', *Teaching Politics*, vol. 3, no. 3.
Jaros, D. (1973), *Socialisation to Politics*, Nelson.
Jennings, M. K. and Niemi, R. G. (1971), *The Political Character of Adolescence*, Princeton University Press.
Joseph, Sir K. (1976), 'Education, Politics and Society', *Teaching Politics*, vol. 5, no. 1.
Karabel, J. and Halsey, A. H. (eds.) (1977), *Power and Ideology in Education*, Oxford University Press.
Kavanagh, D. (1971), 'The Deferential English: a Comparative Critique', *Government and Opposition*, vol. 6, no. 3.
—— (1972), *Political Culture*, Macmillan.

Kazamias, A. M. and Massialas, B. G. (1965), *Tradition and Change in Education*, Prentice Hall.

Kellas, J. G. (1975), *The Scottish Political System* (2nd edn), Cambridge University Press.

Kilbrandon, Lord (chmn) (1973), *Royal Commission on the Constitution, 1969–73*: vol. I, *Report*; vol. II *Memorandum of Dissent*, Cmd 5460–1, HMSO.

King, A. (ed.) (1976), *Why Britain is Becoming Harder to Govern*, BBC Publications.

Klein, J. (1965), *Samples from English Culture*, Routledge and Kegan Paul.

Kogan, M. (1978), *The Politics of Educational Change*, Fontana.

Labour Party (1979), *The Labour Party Manifesto, 1979*.

Lane, R. E. (1972), *Political Man*, Free Press.

Langeveld, W. (1979), *Political Education for Teenagers*, Council for Cultural Co-operation, Council of Europe, Strasbourg.

Langton, K. (1969), *Political Socialisation*, Oxford University Press.

Langton, K. P. and Jennings, M. K. (1968), 'Political Socialisation and the High School Civics Curriculum', *American Political Science Review*, vol. 62.

Lapping, B. and Percy, N. (eds.) (1973), *The State of the Nation: Parliament*, Granada Television.

Laski, H. J. (1938), *A Grammar of Politics* (4th edn), Allen and Unwin.

Lasswell, H. D. (1966), *Analysis of Political Behaviour: an Empirical Approach*, Routledge and Kegan Paul.

Lawton, D. (1968), 'Social Science in Schools', *New Society*, 25 April 1968.

—— (1973), *Social Change, Educational Theory and Curriculum Planning*, University of London Press.

—— (1975), *Class, Culture and the Curriculum*, Routledge and Kegan Paul.

—— (1978), *Education and Social Justice*, Sage.

Lawton, D. and Dufour, B. (1973), *The New Social Studies*, Heinemann.

Leonard, D. (975), *Paying for Politics: the Case for Public Subsidies*, Political and Economic Planning.

Lister, I. (1969), 'Political Education and the Schools', *New University*, vol. 3, no. 3.

—— (1973a), 'The School as a Political Educator', *Socialist Commentary*, September 1973.

—— (1973b), 'Education, Politics and a Vision of Man: a Conversation with Paulo Freire', *The Times Higher Education Supplement*, 13 July 1973.

—— (1977a), 'The Aims and Methods of Political Education and Schools' (paper presented to the Conference on the Development of Democratic Institutions in Europe, organised by the Parliamentary Assembly of the Council of Europe, and held in Strasbourg, April 1976), *Teaching Politics*, vol. 6, no. 1.

—— (1977b), *Report of Political Education Research Unit*, University of York.

Low, S. (1914), *The Governance of England* (revd edn), Ernest Benn.

Luard, E. (1980), *Socialism at the Grassroots*, Fabian Tract no. 468, Fabian Society.

Lucas, J. R. (1976), *Democracy and Participation*, Penguin.

Lupton, T. and Wilson, S. (1969), 'The Social Background and Connections of Top Decision Makers', in R. Rose (ed.), *Policy-Making in Britain*, Macmillan.

McClosky, H. (1969), *Political Inquiry*, Collier-Macmillan.

McDowell, D. (1971), 'The Values of Teacher Education', in T. Burgess (ed.), *Dear Lord James*, Penguin.

McKenzie, R. T. and Silver, A. (1968), *Angels in Marble: Working Class Conservatives in Urban England*, Heinemann.

Mackenzie, W. J. M. (1967), *Politics and Social Science*, Penguin.

Mackintosh, J. P. (1977a), *The Government and Politics of Britain* (4th edn), Hutchinson.

—— (1977b), *Inside British Politics*, Granada Television.

Maclure, J. S. (1965), *Educational Documents 1916–1963*, Chapman and Hall.

Mannheim, K. (1936), *Ideology and Utopia* (tr. L. Wirth and E. Schek), Routledge and Kegan Paul.

—— (1940), *Man and Society in an Age of Reconstruction*, Routledge and Kegan Paul.

—— (1943), *Diagnosis of Our Time*, Routledge and Kegan Paul.

—— (1951), *Freedom, Power and Democratic Planning*, Routledge and Kegan Paul.

—— (1963), *Ideology and Utopia* (tr. L. Wirth and E. Schek), Routledge and Kegan Paul.

Mannheim, K. and Stewart. W. A. C. (1962), *An Introduction to the Sociology of Education*, Routledge and Kegan Paul.

Marcuse, H. (1976), 'Repressive Tolerance', in P. Connerton (ed.), *Critical Sociology*, Penguin.

Massialas, B. G. (1969), *Education and the Political System*, Addison-Welsey.

Mead, M. (1935), *Sex and Temperament in Three Primitive Societies*, Routledge and Kegan Paul.

—— (1942), *Growing up in New Guinea*, Penguin.

—— (1943), *Coming of Age in Samoa*, Penguin.

Mehlinger, H. (1967), *The Study of American Political Behaviour*, High School Curriculum Centre in Government, Indiana University.

Mercer, G. (1972), 'Political Interests among Adolescents: the Influence of Formal Political Education', *Teaching Politics*, vol. 1, no. 1.

——(1973), *Political Education and Socialisation to Democratic Norms*. Occasional Paper no. 11, University of Strathclyde.

Miliband, R. (1976), 'Teaching Politics in an Age of Crisis', *The Times Higher Education Supplement*, 19 March 1976.

Mills, J. S. (1910), *Representative Government*, Everyman.

Miller, J. D. B. (1965), *The Nature of Politics*, Penguin.

Milsom, F. (1978a), *Handbook – Section G.2, Political Education for Church Youth Groups*, Methodist Association of Youth Clubs.

—— (1978b), 'Confusion about Political Education', *Social Services Quarterly*, Winter 1978.

—— (1980), *Political Education: a Practical Guide for Christian Youth*, Paternoster Press.

Ministry of Education (1947), *The New Secondary Education*, Pamphlet no. 9, HMSO.
—— (1949), *Citizens Growing Up*, Pamphlet no. 16, HMSO.
—— (1952), *Teaching History*, Pamphlet no. 23, HMSO.
—— (1959), *15 to 18: a Report of the Central Advisory Council for Education, England, vol. 1*, HMSO.
—— (1963), *Half Our Future: a Report of the Central Advisory Council for Education, England*, HMSO.
Mitchell, A. (1979), *Can Labour Win Again?*, Fabian Tract no. 463, Fabian Society.
Mitter, W. (1972), 'Political Education in West and East (with special reference to the Federal Republic of Germany and the German Democratic Republic)', in K. Smart (ed.), *Education and Politics Report of a Conference held at University of Edinburgh*, Comparative Education Society in Europe.
More, St Thomas (n.d.), *Utopia* (tr. C. J. Collins), Clarendon Press.
Morris-Jones, W. H. (1964), 'In Defence of Apathy', *Political Studies*, vol. 2, no. 1.
Musgrove, F. and Taylor, P. H. (1969), *Society and the Teacher's Role*, Routledge and Kegan Paul.
Nisbet, R. (1976), *The Twilight of Authority*, Heinemann.
Nordlinger, B. A. (1967), *The Working Class Tories*, McGibbon and Kee.
Oakeshott, M. (1962), *Rationalism in Politics and Other Essays*, Methuen.
Ottaway, A, K. C. (1957), *Education and Society*, Routledge and Kegan Paul.
Parry, G. (ed.) (1972), *Participation in Politics*, Manchester University Press.
Pateman, C. (1970), *Participation and Democratic Theory*, Cambridge University Press.
—— (1979), *The Problem of Political Obligation*, Wiley.
Peterson, A. D. C. (1960), *Arts and Science in the Sixth Form*, Department of Education, University of Oxford.
Phenix, P. H. (1964), *Realms of Meaning*, McGraw Hill.
Pickles, D. (1970), *Democracy*, Batsford.
Plato (1945), *Republic* (tr. F. M. Cornford), Oxford University Press.
Punnett, R. M. (1976), *British Government and Politics* (3rd edn), Heinemann.
Pye, L. W. (1965), 'Political Culture and Political Development', in L. W. Pye and S. Verba (eds.), *Political Culture and Political Development*, Princeton University Press.
Radice, G. (1980), *Community Socialism*, Fabian Tract no. 464, Fabian Society.
Renshaw, P. (1973), 'Socialisation: The Negation of Education', *Journal of Moral Education*, vol. 3, no. 3.
Rich, R. W. (1950), *The Teacher in a Planned Society*, University of London Press.
Robson, W. A. (1967), *Politics and Government*, Allen and Unwin.
Rogers, R. (1979), 'The Cold War Comes to School', *New Stateman*, 6 July 1979.
Rose, R. (1974), *Politics in England Today*, Faber and Faber.
—— (1976), *Studies in British Politics* (3rd edn), Macmillan.

Rousseau, J.-J. (n.d.) *The Social Contract* (tr. C. Frankel), Matner Publishing Co.
—— (1953), 'Considerations on the Government of Poland', in F. Watkins (ed.), *Political Writings*, Nelson.
Rust, W. B. (1974), *European Curriculum Studies: no. 9, Social and Civic Education*, Council for Cultural Co-operation, Council of Europe, Strasbourg.
Rutter, M., Maugham, B., Mortimore, P. and Ouston, J. (1979), *Fifteen Thousand Hours: Secondary Schools and their Effects on Children*, Open Books.
Sartori, G. (1962), *Democratic Theory*, Wayne State University Press.
Schleicher, K. (1965), *Politische Bildung in England, 1939–1963*, Quelle Mayer.
Schools Council (1965), *Raising the School Leaving Age*, Working Paper no. 3, HMSO.
—— (1975), *The Whole Curriculum, 13–16*, Working Paper no. 53, Evans/Methuen.
Schwartz, D. C. and Schwartz, S. K. (1975), *New Directions in Political Socialisation*, Free Press.
Seymour-Ure, C. (1974), *The Political Impact of Mass Media*, Constable.
Skeffington, A. (chmn) (1969), *People and Planning; Report of the Committee on Public Participation in Planning*, HMSO.
Simon, B. (1965), *Education and the Labour Movement*, Lawrence and Wishart.
Smart, K. (ed.) (1972), *Education and Politics: Report of a Conference held at University of Edinburgh*, Comparative Education Society in Europe, British Section.
Snook, I. A. (1972a), *Concepts of Indoctrination: Philosophic Essays*, Routledge and Kegan Paul.
—— (1972b), *Indoctrination and Education*, Routledge and Kegan Paul.
Stanworth, P. and Giddens, A. (eds.) (1974), *Elites and Power in British Society*, Cambridge University Press.
Stenhouse, L. (1967), *Culture and Education*, Nelson.
Stewart, W. A. C. (1953), 'Karl Mannheim and the Sociology of Education', *British Journal of Educational Studies*, vol. 1, no. 2.
—— (1967), *Karl Mannheim on Education and Social Thought*, Harrap for University of London.
St John Stevas, N. (1977), 'Political Education in Schools', Speech to Birmingham Bow Group, 18 November 1977, Conservative Central Office.
Storm, M. (1971), 'Schools and the Community, an Issue-based Approach', *Bulletin of Environmental Education*, vol. 1, no. 1.
Stradling, R. E. (1977), *The Political Awareness of the School Leaver*, Hansard Society.
—— (1979), *Political Education: Recent Theory, Practice and Research*, Information Series no. 2, Politics Association.
Studdert-Kennedy, G. (1978), 'Political Socialisation', *Teaching Politics*, vol. 7, no. 2.

132   *Bibliography*

Sutton, J. S. (1977), 'Parliament, the Public and Political Education', *Teaching Politics*, vol. 6, no. 1.
Tapper, T. (1971), *Young People and Society*, Faber and Faber.
—— (1975), 'The Limits of Political Education: an Expanding Interest', *Teaching Politics*, vol. 4, no. 1.
Tapper, T. and Salter, B. (1978), *Education and the Political Order*, Macmillan.
Taylor, W. (1969), *Society and the Education of Teachers*, Faber and Faber.
Torney, W. V., Oppenhiem, A. N. and Farnen, R. F. (1975), *Civic Education in Ten Countries*, John Wiley.
Trilling, L. (1953), *The Liberal Imagination*, Doubleday.
Tyler, R. (1949), *Basic Principles of Curriculum and Instruction*, University of Chicago Press.
Tyler, W. (1977), *The Sociology of Educational Inequality*, Methuen.
Tylor, E. B. (1871), *Primitive Culture*, Holt.
Ungar, R. M. (1976), *Knowledge and Politics*, Free Press.
University of London (1977), *General Certificate of Education: Advanced Level Government and Political Studies*.
Urry, J. and Wakeford, J. (eds.) (1973), *Power in Britain*, Heinemann.
Wake, R. A., Marbeau, V. and Peterson, A. D. C. (1979), *Innnovation in Secondary Education*, Council for Cultural Co-operation, Council of Europe, Strasbourg.
Wakeford, J. (1969), *Cloistered Elite*, Macmillan.
Walsh, W. (1959), *The Use of Imagination*, Chatto and Windus.
Ward, L. O. (1974), 'Political Socialisation and the Schools', *Teaching Politics*, vol. 3, no. 1.
Webb, J. (1962), 'The Sociology of a School', *British Journal of Sociology*, vol. 13, no. 3.
Welsh, W. A. (1973), *Studying Politics*, Nelson.
Westergaard, J. and Resler, H. (1976), *Class in a Capitalist Society*, Penguin.
White, J. P. (1973), *Towards a Compulsory Curriculum*, Routledge and Kegan Paul.
—— (1979), 'Socialist Perspectives on the Curriculum', in R. Rubinstein (ed.), *Education and Inequality*, Penguin.
White, P. A. (1972), 'Socialisation and Education', in R. F. Dearden, P. H. Hirst and R. S. Peters (eds.), *Education and the Development of Reason*, Routledge and Kegan Paul.
—— (1977), 'Political Education in a Democracy: the Implications for Teacher Education', *Journal of Further and Higher Education*, vol. 1, no. 3.
Whitmarsh, G. (1974), 'The Politics of Political Education: an Episode', *Journal of Curriculum Studies*, vol. 6, no. 2.
Whitty, G. (1978), 'Political Education in Schools', *Socialism and Education*, vol. 5, no. 5.
Wilkinson, R. (1964), *The Prefects: British Leadership and the Public School Tradition*, Oxford University Press.
Williams, R. (1961), *The Long Revolution*, Penguin.

Willis, P. E. (1976), 'The Class Significance of School Counter-Culture', in
  M. Hammersly and P. Woods (eds), *The Process of Schooling*, Routledge
  and Kegan Paul/Open University.
—— (1977), *Learning to Labour*, Saxon House.
Wiseman, H. V. (1966), *Politics in Everyday Life*, Blackwell.
Wrong, D. H. (1961), 'The Over-socialized Conception of Man', *American
  Sociological Review*, vol. 26, no. 2.
Young, M. and Whitty, G. (eds.) (1977), *Society, State and Schooling*, Falmer
  Press.

Appendix I

The need for political education in Britain (A policy statement discussed and endorsed by the 1980 National Conference of the Politics Association)

Background and aims

The Politics Association was founded in 1969 at a conference sponsored by the Hansard Society for Parliamentary Government in order to provide a professional service for those actively engaged or interested in the teaching of politics at every level of the educational system.

The Association is concerned both with the teaching of politics as an academic subject and the process of political education within society. It has been closely associated with the Hansard Society in major research projects, most notably, *A Programme for Political Education*, sponsored by the Nuffield Foundation and the Schools Council, and a survey of *The Political Awareness of Young School Leavers*, supported by the Leverhulme Trust. The latter reinforced the Kilbrandon Report on the Constitution by drawing attention to a disturbing degree of political ignorance, cynicism and apathy in our population.

At a time when government decisions impinge increasingly upon our lives and social issues are ever more complex, it is clear that a large proportion of young people, due to receive the vote at 18, are leaving school almost devoid of any effective education in the politics of Britain. The Politics Association believes that this situation reflects a widespread failure to provide relevant and effective forms of political education by our schools and colleges, by government, and by public voluntary institutions such as political parties and trade unions. Unless serious efforts are made to remedy this situation, political alienation is likely to increase in intensity until the viability of our political system itself is fundamentally threatened.

Political literacy

The Association believes that in order to combat growing disillusion with the democratic process, urgent advances are necessary

in what the Programme for Political Education called *Political Literacy*. By political literacy is meant a compound of knowledge, skills and attitudes which will enable an individual to be politically effective. At the most fundamental level a politically literate person will possess the basic information necessary to understand political problems and will have the confidence and ability to contribute towards their resolution should he choose to do so. He will be capable of something more than enlightened self-interest; he will realise the effects of his actions upon others and will understand their different viewpoints. More precisely, political literacy means:
– a critical awareness and understanding of our system of government
– widespread knowledge of the important issues of the day
– the ability of individuals to participate in the political process
– a general acceptance that it is perfectly legitimate for others to hold and pursue political views and policies different from one's own
– the recognition that in an interdependent society political problems must be resolved by rational debate within the framework of law.

Recommendations

1   The Politics Association believes that the need for political education must be recognised by the government, political parties and educational authorities and institutions as a *key priority*.

2   The Association welcomes the DES initiative on moves towards reaching an agreement on a *common-core curriculum* and believes strongly that *political education must be accorded a distinctive role within it*. Moreover, the Association believes that politics as an academic subject should be available as a series of optional studies beyond the core curriculum in all secondary schools.

3   The Association also takes the view that schools which are genuinely concerned to prepare citizens for life in a democratic society should be encouraged to examine the *educational possibilities inherent in their own organisations* in an effort to realise this end.

4   The Association recognises that the implementation of a thorough-going development in political education will have important repercussions on *teacher training institutions*. It recommends that urgent consideration be given to the need to establish *relevant courses of academic and professional study* both at the initial and inservice levels.

5   Whilst highly appreciative of funds so far provided by the DES and certain other bodies, the Association recommends that finance should be provided for *further research to improve the possibilities of effective political learning*. It also recommends that the fullest consideration should be given to research and experiments in political

education conducted in youth organisations and informal settings.

6   The Politics Association recognises that the spread of political
literacy cannot be achieved by the schools alone. If this aim is taken
seriously it will require the co-operation of a whole range of
governmental institutions and voluntary organisations. It recommends that, wherever possible, *government bodies* should follow the
example of the House of Commons in appointing a full or part-time
education officer responsible for liaison with schools and the dissemi-
nation of appropriate information to young people. Political parties,
trade unions, the CBI and other voluntary public bodies are urged
to *extend and improve* internal education in politics for their own
members and for the rest of society.

7   Television and radio have made substantial contributions to
the advancement of political education. However, high-quality programmes apart, there is a tendency to personalise important political
issues or to offer programmes which are too specialised to advance
the political literacy of the majority. The Association strongly
recommends *programme planners and makers* to use their expertise and
flair to produce programmes which explain the political system and
show how it can be made to respond to the needs and interests of
all groups in society.

Tom Brennan – *Chairman*
Bill Jones – *Vice Chairman*

Appendix II

Text agreed by the three main political parties on the controversy about politics in schools

Agreement in politics row

Preface

(a)   On the initiative of the Politics Association (which is a professional association of teachers in Secondary and Further Education concerned with political and civic education) a meeting was held with representatives of the three main political parties on the premises of the Hansard Society. (Professor Bernard Crick took the chair on behalf of the Politics Assocation and the Chairman, Mr Derek Heater, also attended; Mr John Selwyn Gummer, MP, represented the Conservative Party, Mr Frank Underhill, the national agent, represented the Labour Party and Mr John Pardoe, MP, the Liberal Party; Mr Richard Tames attended as observer for the Hansard Society, being their Research and Development Officer.)

This following statement is simply a letter of advice prepared by the Politics Association to be sent to its members and l.e.a.s which attempts to establish conventions and voluntary rules by which schools may invite politicians to visit during school time to talk about public affairs of any kind likely to prove controversial even if not directly partisan, or by which schools may release pupils to attend such meetings in school time.

Following discussion, the representatives of the parties wish to associate themselves with the following recommendations.

The representatives of the political parties also agreed that they would hold further discussions with the Politics Association to explore an experimental programme in the schools with a view to improving and developing the role of the parties in civic education.

(b)   The problem of the school-leaver, especially at the sixth-form age, is particularly sensitive because, of course, of the vote at 18. Parties will now be seeking more than ever before to inform and influence incipient young voters. The Politics Association considers that this is wholly proper and should form part of a civic education, provided that schools retain fundamental control of the process and that certain conventions are observed. We fear that the result of the recent controversy could be to make some l.e.a.s and head teachers even more restrictive than a few already are – practices appear to vary widely – about visits from or to politicians. We wish to avert this, indeed to try to get more visits rather than less, but in an educationally meaningful way.

(c)   Civic education, whether in CSE, O or A-level syllabuses as British Constitution or Government and Politics, or in sixth-form General, Liberal or Social Studies time, is both a highly important and a difficult, hence sometimes neglected area. It needs expansion and more thought both for its educational value and as a deliberate attempt to make young people aware of their responsibilities as citizens, which obviously must include the possibility of supporting and even joining political parties and pressure groups. We deeply fear the social consequences if over-direct approaches to schools by the parties make this whole area too controversial for schools to handle. The suppression of political controversy can lead to the rejection of politics, sometimes in forms more worrying than mere apathy.

(d)   Suspicion that civic education is partisan would tend to drive out the good with the bad. Obviously the political parties will seek to play a more direct role in civic education with votes at eighteen, but obviously if schools are not to close down the shutters the parties must themselves help to observe some such rules of prudence or conventions as the following. Therefore we suggest:

Recommendations
1   That politicians talking to pupils on controversial matters in school time should only do so in circumstances where they fit into a systematic programme organised by the school or group of schools and when there has been preparation by the teachers. Isolated visits tend, we suggest, to be a waste of everyone's time, and schools should not think that their responsibilities for civic education are met simply by talks from the parties: they must be prepared for and followed up afterwards by the schools.
2   That there is a place both for the balanced panel discussion and for a talk by one or more speakers from one party. But if the latter, then in commonsense and prudence, we suggest that no invitation should be given or accepted without it being announced at the same time that a similar invitation has been given to or accepted from one of the other main parties; and that in the long run there should be balance-over-time between the parties. In all circumstances ample

time must be guaranteed for questions; and if a panel, then schools should realise that fairly large numbers are needed to justify the presence of leading local (let alone national) spokesmen of the parties together. Pedagogically, we have some sympathy with the view that panel discussions can be overdone, encourage more debate and often leave little time for questions and discussion from the audience; but obviously there is a place for both, and we see no reason why speakers from one party should not meet pupils on their own so long as balance-over-time is observed (and the relevant time is the school year).

3   That so long as balance within a meeting or balance-over-time is observed, we see no issue of principle whether meetings are within a school or held outside, but if held within a school for that school alone, then balance-over-time must be interpreted school by school and not district by district. Meetings organised by heads or assistant teachers immediately after school hours on school premises should, we think, follow the same rules of prudence and public interest about balance. Where there are sixth-form political or public affairs clubs, run by the pupils on school premises, the question is somewhat different, although schools should be well aware that the public do not always find the distinction easy to draw, and balance should also be striven for in this context.

4   That it is clearly the responsibility of school heads and l.e.a.s to ensure that meetings, whosoever they are organised by, which pupils attend in or from schools are either genuinely non-partisan, multi-party or fit into a programme which is balanced between the parties over the school year. We are firmly of the opinion that meetings organised by single parties, on whatever subject, will inevitably be regarded as partisan.

5   That the kind of meetings envisaged in this document should, we believe, ordinarily be held on the initiative or by the permission of individual head teachers or groups of head teachers. The role of the chief education officer or the education committee is best limited to ensuring that balance is maintained over time by retrospective scrutiny, not by prior permission for every invitation of a politician to a school or groups of schools. We are aware that present practices vary widely in this respect.

6   That the local constituency MP is in a special position. Nowhere more than in schools does he ordinarily remember that he is representative of all the people in his constituency. We simply hope that the local MP will remember the danger to civic education as such of engendering controversy about 'politics in schools'. Also in a special position are individual invitations to acknowledged authorities on the machinery of government, the organisation of the

parties and the procedures of Parliament, even though they are politicians.

7   That, despite the recent controversies, we note continual difficulties of schoolteachers to get party spokesmen to talk in schools and that this sometimes affects balance. There is some lack of realism in teachers asking the same individuals too often, and there is also some lack of knowledge about how to approach the parties as organisations, particularly in the regions. But the parties could do more to inform schools about the availability of speakers, or simply to acknowledge a responsibility to find local spokesmen when asked.

8   That non-partisan outside bodies could play a greater role in organising sixth-form conferences in public affairs and on controversial matters. The Council for Education in World Citizenship (affiliated to the United Nations Association) already does much excellent work for schools in the field of international understanding. But we think that issues of domestic politics can also be handled in this way, and both the Hansard Society for Parliamentary Government and the Politics Association have considerable experience in organising sixth-form conferences (although these have been mainly limited, for lack of funds and personnel, to the London area). We also remind schools that on such occasions university and polytechnic teachers and journalists have often made useful contributions in addition to politicians. All three bodies stand ready to advise, organise or sponsor future meetings, within the limits of their resources, and already enjoy good informal contacts with the parties.

9   That there is a similar problem with minority groups and pressure groups that is partly met by the same considerations of balance-over-time, but also could be partly met if the practice were more widespread of having sixth form noticeboards. These could be used to display circulars, relating to meetings outside school hours, couched in reasonable terms and issued by outside bodies – whether parties or pressure groups. This is, we know, a small but sensitive matter of head teachers' discretion but with votes at 18 and the increased activity of local pressure groups, we would suggest that a non-official notice board is less nuisance than continual leafleting by outside bodies at school gates.

(From *The Times Educational Supplement*, 2 February 1973)

Appendix III

Political education and *A Framework for the School Curriculum*

I *Introduction*

1 The Politics Association welcomes the opportunity to respond to the proposals outlined in *A Framework for the School Curriculum* (DES, 1980) and wishes to offer its views on the place of political education in the curriculum of the secondary school.

2 It hopes that these observations can be carefully considered prior to the publication of the more definitive statement which is to provide further guidance for local authorities, schools and teachers.

3 In compiling these observations reference has been made to the following related documents:

(i) *Curriculum 11–16: Working Papers by HM Inspectors*, DES, 1979

(ii) *Aspects of Secondary Education in England: A Survey by HM Inspectors*, HMSO, 1979

(iii) *Local Authority Arrangements for the School Curriculum: Report on the Circular 14/77 Review*, HMSO, 1979

(iv) *A View of the Curriculum*, HMSO, 1980

II *Summary of observations*

1 The Association's comments are detailed below but, for convenience, the more important points made are included in summary form here.

2 The Politics Association:

2.1 Welcomes the inclusive definition of the curriculum and the recognition of the way in which what is intended by the school can be adversely affected by the 'hidden' curriculum (III 1–3)

2.2 welcomes the initiative of the Secretaries of State in seeking a national consensus on a desirable framework for the curriculum (IV 1)

2.3 supports the view that LEAs should consider the ways in which schools should prepare pupils for adult responsibilities (IV 2)

2.4 supports the belief that an appropriate selection from our complex culture can best be experienced in the school through a common core curriculum which reflects the important relevant 'areas of experience' (IV 4–5)

2.5 welcomes the specific inclusion of the 'social and political' area of experience and the principle that all of these areas are of equal importance (IV 6–7)

2.6 suggests certain criteria against which the effectiveness of political education in schools can be assessed (V 1–2)

2.7 expresses some reservations about the approach to political education through traditional subjects as a general strategy (VI 4–5)

2.8 recognises increasing support for the view that political education should be a clearly identifiable element within social science or social studies courses or within 'integrated studies' programmes, but draws attention to the existence of other approaches and the desirability of continuing experiment within this field (VI 6–7)

2.9 regrets the apparent reluctance of some schools and LEAs to accept the desirability of providing an effective form of political education (VI 1–2, 5)

2.10 draws attention to the importance of creating an atmosphere and attitudes in the classroom and in the school which are conducive to political education (VI 10)

2.11 urges the provision of necessary resources and stresses the need to develop teacher training and research in this field (VII 1–2)

2.12 draws attention to the contribution which agencies other than the school could make in contributing to the development of political education (VII 3)

III *The school and the curriculum*

1   The Association welcomes the inclusive definition of the curriculum contained in *A View of the Curriculum*, viz:

The curriculum in its full sense comprises all the opportunities for learning provided by a school. It includes the formal programme of lessons in the timetable; the so-called 'extra-curricular' and 'out of school' activities deliberately promoted or supported by the school; and the climate of relationships, attitudes, styles of behaviour and the general quality of life established in the school community as a whole. (p. 2)

2   It also welcomes the recognition, expressed most specifically in *Curriculum 11–16*, that 'curricula give out messages' and that 'in any curriculum the selection of subjects and skills to be taught and the attitudes and activities that are encouraged implies certain political and social assumptions and values, however unconscious.' (p. 10)

3   The Association have noted the HMIs' clear awareness of the power of the 'hidden curriculum' and what the French call 'the parallel school' (pp. 12–13). It wishes to underline this important consideration and to emphasise the danger that, unless suitable safeguards are made, these influences can detract seriously from the realisation of the formally expressed aims of the curriculum. This, we suggest, applies with particular force in the area of political and social education.

IV *A common core curriculum*

1 The Politics Association welcomes the announcement by the Secretaries of State that it is their intention to seek a national consensus on a desirable framework for the school curriculum. It recognises that 'they have an inescapable duty to satisfy themselves that the work of schools matches national needs'. (*A Framework for the School Curriculum*, p. 1.) but urges that this duty should not be viewed in unduly narrow economic terms. We assume that the concept of national needs also embraces fundamental political and social requirements and that due regard will continue to be paid to the tradition of a liberal education and a concern for individual self-realisation.

2 The Association agrees that all concerned need to consider 'the extent to which some key subjects should be regarded as essential components of the curriculum for all pupils' and 'the ways in which the curriculum, whatever subject structure may be adopted, should seek to prepare pupils for employment and adult responsibilities in society'. (p. 2) It considers that a clear recognition of the political dimension of human experience is essential to the realisation of this objective.

3 It accepts that: 'Schools are likely to be more effective in achieving their curricular aims if these aims are set out clearly in writing, are generally known and accepted by staff and pupils, and are sympathetically pursued through curriculum organisation and day-to-day teaching.' (p. 2)

4 The Association welcomes the assertion that pupils in school are the inheritors of a complex culture and that 'they have nothing less than a right to be introduced to a selection of its essential elements.' (*Curriculum 11–16*, p. 5) It believes that the way in which this 'selection from culture' can be best experienced in the school situation is through the existence of a common core curriculum which comprises 'perhaps as much as two-thirds or three-quarters of the time available'. (*Curriculum 11–16*, p. 6) It is in full agreement with Proposition 2 in *A View of the Curriculum* which suggests that: '"Secondary Education for All" entails that the formal curriculum should offer all pupils opportunities to engage in a largely comparable range of learning.' (p. 14)

5   The Association endorses the eight 'areas of experience' designated in *Curriculum 11–16* (and subsequent publications) as a desirable and satisfactory categorisation of the necessary 'selection from culture' viz: 'the aesthetic and creative, the ethical, the linguistic, the mathematical, the physical, the scientific, the social and political, and the spiritual'. It recognises that each of these areas reflects particular perspectives and emphases of necessary concern but also that, within the curriculum, there are opportunities of mutual reference and reinforcement between the areas. Thus, social and political education must have reference to ethical and linguistic considerations but neither of these can, of themselves, ensure the realisation of the objectives of the social and political area of experience.

6   The Politics Association welcomes the specific inclusion of the social and political area of experience not least because of the neglect of this dimension of educational thought and practice for a long period of time and because it is capable of providing in the curriculum a practical and modernising element in an area which has previously been rejected or ignored.

7   The Association would, however, wish to underline the principle that all of these areas of 'of equal importance' (*Curriculum 11–16*, p. 6) and would wish to guard against the possibility that the essential requirements of this area are not overlooked in over-preoccupation with the more traditional areas of the curriculum. It believes that a similar danger exists in the tendency in some publications to subsume the social and political area of experience within more general groupings such as 'Preparation for Adult and Working Life' and 'Social Education' (see e.g. *A Framework for the School Curriculum*, pp. 4–8) and the various forms of moral education. The Association believes that where the curriculum requires a new emphasis, as is the case with social and political education, it is all the more important that the nature of the new requirement is clearly and consistently spelled out.

   IV   *Tests of effectiveness for political education*
1   The Politics Association agrees that 'the curriculum should be capable of demonstrating that it offers properly thought out and progressive experience in all of these areas'. (*Curriculum 11–16*, p. 6) and that the curriculum and work of school should be judged by 'the effectiveness with which they contribute to this achievement'. (*A Framework for the School Curriculum*, p. 3)

2   The Association suggests that the following criteria might be usefully employed in assessing the effectiveness or otherwise of the provision for political education in the secondary school.

(i)   Does political education have an adequate and identifiable place as an essential 'area of experience' within the common core curriculum?

(ii)   Does the scheme of work reflect a concern to develop the kind of knowledge, attitudes and skills advocated in the HMIs' paper on 'Political Competence' (*Curriculum 11–16*, pp. 56–8) and the notion of political literacy advanced in the Report of the Hansard Society Programme for Political Education (B. Crick and A. Porter, eds., *Political Education and Political Literacy*, Longman, 1978)?

(iii)   Is the political dimension of *other* areas of experience within the curriculum adequately recognised and represented?

(iv)   To what extent does the organisation of the school itself enhance or hinder opportunities for constructive political learning?

(v)   To what extent are the teaching styles employed conducive to the encouragement of relevant knowledge, attitudes and skills?

(vi)   Does the allocation of staff and resources within the school ensure that due weight is given to political education?

(vii)   Is the provision for political education broadly comparable for all groups within the school?

(viii) Beyond the core curriculum, is politics as an academic subject available as an *optional* study?

VI   *Political education and the curriculum*

1   The Politics Association accepts that: 'A common policy for the curriculum...cannot be a prescription for uniformity.' (*A View of the Curriculum*, p. 2) Nevertheless, it is clearly important that realistic efforts are made to achieve agreed objectives and there must be more than mere token compliance with the need to implement the principles of 'coverage' and 'balance' within the curriculum.

2   So far as political education is concerned recent practice reflects three main types of aproach, viz:

(i)   the inclusion of politics as a separate subject

(ii)   the inclusion of political education within social science or social studies, or with 'integrated studies' or 'humanities' programmes

(iii)   the attempted realisation of political education objectives through the medium of one of the more traditional subjects.

3   The Association is aware that, in the hands of an informed and experienced teacher, practical education can be effectively undertaken through the medium of History or English (for example); it has some reservations about this approach as a general strategy. Such an approach, we believe, may militate against other desirable and

legitimate aims within the subject concerned and may well result in a failure to devote attention systematically to the requirements of political education. There is a further danger that recourse to this pattern may work against the need to review the curriculum as a whole and present the possibility of a fictitious rather than real provision for certain of the 'areas of experience' regarded as desirable. The existence of an identifiable place for political education may also serve best in allaying the frequently expressed fears of bias and indoctrination.

4   The Association, therefore, does not accept the view expressed in *Curriculum 11–16* that: 'Social objectives do not require the introduction of new subjects into the curriculum. Most of the necessary knowledge can be transmitted through established subjects or a combination of them.' (p. 13) History, for example, may be a necessary condition for political understanding, but it is not, of itself, a sufficient condition.

5   The Association is impressed by the efforts made in a number of schools and local authorities to provide effective patterns of political education. It is clear, however, that in some parts of the country there is considerable reluctance to embrace this important development in the curriculum. The Association is concerned that, in response to the question in Circular 14/77 'What steps have the authority taken to help schools promote the development in their pupils of a basic understanding of contemporary economic, social and political life?', three-fifths of the LEAs said that the issues underlying the question 'could be largely incorporated into more or less traditional subjects' (*Local Authority Arrangements for the School Curriculum*, p. 160). Some authorities 'made particular mention of political education, usually expressing an awareness of the need for caution in introducing it as a separate subject'. (p. 161) 'Less than one tenth of the responses indicated that the authority had designated an adviser with particular responsibility for all or part of the area covered by this question.' (p. 161)

6   A substantial body of opinion both within and outside of the Politics Association takes the view that, on balance, political education should form part of a broader approach to the study of man in society and is best located within the traditions and framework of the Humanities and Social Sciences. It recognises that social, economic, and political concepts are inter-related and that there are considerable advantages in the development of teaching strategies which will enable each of these fields of study to inform and enliven the other. It is equally important, however, that political education is not merged into a wider programme of inter-disciplinary or 'integrated' study to the extent that it loses its identity. The political

education component within the core curriculum must retain a clear focus in the minds of teachers and pupils alike. Whatever form political education takes it must address itself to a particular set of ideas and concepts, examine the nature and working of concrete institutions and organisations and confront current arguments, problems and issues of a political nature. The Politics Association takes the view that there are likely to be a number of viable approaches which, each in its own way, can meet the requirements of political education. Continued experiment with different resources, methods and approaches is desirable and due regard should be paid to existing and developing practices and traditions in both political education and the teaching of politics as an academic subject. The experience gained in various modifications of a more directly institutional approach, public administration courses in colleges of further education, the various forms of 'integrated' studies and social studies, the Scottish Modern Studies courses etc., must be taken carefully into account. The Association hopes that, as this work develops, a systematic appraisal can be made of the advantages and disadvantages of different approaches and methods.

7   The HMIs' paper on 'Political Competence' and the Report of the Hansard Society's Programme for Political Education provide a workable framework for the development of a form of political education which can claim a wide measure of educational and political consensus. The emphasis in these approaches is on the need to develop knowledge, attitudes and skills relevant to political awareness and the capacity to act politically within the traditions of political democracy. This involves 'not so much a study of institutions but of issues, not of constitutional forms but political motivation and the criteria for making political decisions...' (*Curriculum 11–16*, p. 12)

8   The Association also strongly urges that, beyond the common core curriculum, politics as an academic subject at appropriate levels can increasingly be made available either within the school or within a group of schools. Important changes have been made in GCE Advanced Level syllabuses in Government and Politics in recent years and it is hoped that before long similar changes will be introduced for GCE Ordinary Level and CSE courses.

9   The Association also suggests that if, beyond the specific provision for political education within the core curriculum, teachers in other areas of experience are conscious of the social and political dimensions of the particular range of matters with which they are concerned and incorporate these considerations in their teaching, this would make a valuable contribution to the pupils' political education. The HMIs' papers in *Curriculum 11–16* provide excellent guidelines for this

purpose and attention is directed to the example quoted for Classics (p. 46); History (p. 53); Economics (pp. 53–5); Geography (p. 61); and Environmental Education (pp. 71–2).

10   In the Report of the Programme for Political Education (Crick and Porter, 1978), attention was drawn to the need for an atmosphere in the classroom and in the school which is conducive to political education. It was observed that: 'The style of teaching and general atmosphere of the school be versatile, open and reasonably "democratic", that is, enabling considerable student participation in as many aspects of the programme as possible.' Similarly in *Curriculum 11–16* it is suggested that, '...school structures should allow all pupils the possibility of gaining experiences and skills in discussion, argument and decision making'. If the schools are to be genuinely concerned in the preparation of citizens for life in a democratic society, it is important that considerable thought should be given to the educational possibilities inherent in school organisation. Many schools already provide opportunities for gaining experience in a variety of forms of participation and social service and the Association believes that an extension of opportunities for young people for participation in decision-making and social and political involvement in appropriate forms would make a significant contribution to the development of the kind of knowledge, attitudes and skills which are both educationally and politically relevant.

VII   *Implications*

1   The Politics Association recognises that the desiderata for the development of political education outlined above carry with them implications for resource utilisation and staff development. In particular the Association wishes to draw attention to the gross lack of provision for full-time teacher training in this field both at pre-service and in-service levels and the need for research into relevant teaching methods and resources.

2   It is not assumed that the development of political education is dependent on the presence in schools of trained politics graduates, for such an expectation (in the short term at least) is manifestly unrealistic. The Association does, however, urge that a special effort should be made to ensure that a number of specialist teachers in this field become available and that those making significant contributions organisationally and developmentally within the school are suitably recognised in status terms. The Association also urges that non-specialist teachers who have demonstrated interest and expertise in political education should be given opportunities to develop their skills and commitment and should be similarly recognised in the light of the contribution made.

3   The Association recognises that responsibility for the development

of an effective pattern of political education does not rest on the schools alone. Education alone cannot change society and it is probably true that the preservation and strengthening of political democracy can only be achieved if the schools along with other agencies, such as Government, the media, and the political parties, make a serious effort to heighten the level of critical awareness of society, to increase the possibilities of political involvement, and to seek to develop in young people knowledge, attitudes and skills which will enable them to become politically sensitive and to contribute constructively to the process of political and social change. Such a change in governmental, societal and educational practice will, it is hoped, serve two important purposes. It will encourage a renewal of respect for a democratic system which is increasingly being brought into question and provide 'the tools for informed and responsible participation' in its development and renewal.

Tom Brennan
Chairman The Politics Association
May 1980